solving conflict nonviolently

Atrium Publications
PO Box 938
Ojai, CA 93024-0938

Illustrations: Rod Cameron
Design & Production: Charlene Koonce
Cover Design: Robert Howard
Typesetting: I'm Your Type
Editor: Adryan Russ
Advisor: John Shoolery
Creative Consultant: Jean Webster-Doyle

Special thanks to our daughter, Felicity Aine Doyle,
for her tremendous courage and spirit
in coping with the "invisible enemy."
With love, and deepest care and affection,
from all her friends and family.

ISBN: 0-942941-19-5
ISBN: 0-942941-18-7 (Pbk.)

Printed in Hong Kong

FIGHTING THE INVISIBLE ENEMY

UNDERSTANDING THE EFFECTS OF CONDITIONING ON YOUNG PEOPLE

by Terrence Webster Doyle

Atrium Publications
Ojai, California

This book is dedicated to you young people who feel confused by the invisible battles going on within you and would like to understand what causes them. This book is also dedicated to parents, teachers, counselors and school administrators who want to help young people understand the effects of conditioning on their lives and in the world.

Table of Contents

Are You Game to Not Fight?
(An Introduction)

Hello, my name is Terrence Webster-Doyle, and I want you to know that you don't have to fight.

I am a school teacher and Karate instructor, but the Karate I teach is different from the kind you may have seen on TV and in the movies. The Karate I teach is a way to protect yourself, but it also provides ways to deal with threatening situations without fighting: The Karate I teach offers peaceful approaches to solving conflict.

I am writing this book because I don't want you to get hurt. I grew up in a very rough town near New York City, and I was beaten up a lot. World War II was "full on" then, and all the kids played with war toys. We had very real looking guns, like the German Luger and the Colt 45 Automatic. We used to watch war movies and westerns, and John Wayne was one of our heroes. We also played "cowboys and Indians," and I always wanted to be a cowboy, because we believed that cowboys were the "good" guys.

We "good" guys saw ourselves as heroes — all-American G.I. Joes honorably defending our country. In those days, our "enemies" were the Germans and the Japanese; I remember seeing newspaper and magazine drawings depicting them as snakes, or rats with horns — like the devil. I was confused about the Germans being "the enemy" because my mother's family had come from Germany: How could the Germans be my enemy when my mother was German? And I had Japanese friends at school: How could the Japanese be my enemy when I liked so many Japanese people?

1

As a child, I thought war was just a game. As I grew up, I found out that war is very real and its effects devastating. I was taught ("conditioned") to believe that war is necessary, and grew up believing this. Now that I'm an adult, I'm interested in understanding what causes war and what each of us can do to end it.

This book is intended to help you understand conditioning, because I think that what we call "conditioning" is the main cause of conflict — inside us as tension, fear, hate and anger, and outside as war. If we can become aware of how we are "conditioned" in our day-to-day life, then we can understand how such conditioning can lead to world conflict.

Conditioning, and what causes it, is the *"invisible enemy"* because it is often unseen, hidden. The usual approach to dealing with this "enemy" is to fight it — which just makes the situation worse. However, if you can understand conditioning, you can be free of it.

Silence is a Weapon
A Story

You crouch low in the tall grass, your gun hugged close to you. Sweat rolls down your dirty face. The sky is dark, but the air is hot, and your mouth feels dry.

You hear a sudden noise. Is it the enemy? You hope desperately that it's Tom. Where the devil is he? Has he been hurt? You picked him as your partner because he knows the war zone territory better than anyone. He's a super athlete and a strong fighter.

4

Your mind flashes back to when the two of you were small children, and Tom got a complete G.I. outfit for Christmas, with an authentic looking M-16, a pretend grenade, and Special Forces survival gear. He knew every battle ever fought and had the greatest collection of war comics.

Tom was also a computer whiz. Nobody could beat him at the arcade. His favorite games were Phantom Fighter and Hand-to-Hand Combat. Aside from being an excellent target specialist, he was a Martial Artist. The Golden Fist Fighting Academy taught him how to punch, kick and handle weapons. Tom's life goal was to become a soldier of fortune, a professional warrior for hire.

The sound of a voice brings you back to where you are. The voice is calling your code name and is getting closer every second. How can you be sure that the voice is Tom's, and how are you going to capture the hill if this isn't Tom? This "easy" mission is getting more difficult by the minute. The woods ahead are full of maple trees and low bushes — just like the woods where you grew up.

"Code Red, Code Red, where are you?" cries the voice. "Why don't you answer me?"

Something in the voice sounds frightening. It has to be Tom's, but it doesn't sound familiar. Who else would know your code name? Is this a trap? One of those enemy tricks you've heard about? You freeze at the thought that Tom may have been captured and tortured into giving out your secret name.

You reach for your commando knife. The cold steel shocks your sweating hand. You think, "Silence is a weapon. Silence is survival." You inch forward toward the voice. Unwarlike thoughts race through your brain: "Who is this enemy? Why does he want to hurt me? He's a human being just like me. Why do I want to hurt him?"

You remember seeing pictures of the enemy: short, squat, with dark hair and eyes, and the look of a rat — a devil in human form. The terrorists: the Ivans and Changs, the Tojos and Ishmaels — the foreign invaders. And you remember seeing the images of your hero, Sergeant Armstrong: big, muscular, square jaw, blond crew cut and steely blue-gray eyes. Sergeant Armstrong's mission is to save the world for freedom, to defend against the enemies of peace: the terrorists who support Totalitarianism and worship a God of War. Sergeant Armstrong's Sword of Truth is his M-16. His Shield of Honor is the tank battalion he commands. Everyone knows Sergeant Armstrong is a *real* soldier — true blue, forged from blood, sweat and tears.

Suddenly you see yourself at the beach playing with your friends. You can smell the sea air, see the clear blue sky, and feel the fresh salt water against your body as you jump the waves. Your friends are all there: Solomon, Yuki, Muhammed, Gretchen. A bird flaps its wings and... click! Suddenly you hear the sound of a gun being cocked. You can smell the decay and feel the danger. Your muscles tense and your eyes strain to see in the darkness. You want to run away. You wish you could go home. Is this for real? Weren't you just playing soldiers around your neighborhood? Didn't Tom just come by, and you were going to...

Suddenly, a large black figure jumps out of the night and charges at you, screaming war cries in a language you've never heard. For a second, you are stunned, frozen in terror. Then your training comes into play. Your hand pulls out the knife as you leap forward to meet your attacker. But you're a second too late. There is a sudden blinding white light, catching you and your attacker in a timeless moment — as if a gigantic flash photograph has been taken. You are suddenly in your classroom back in school, standing with some of your platoon buddies. Mrs. Johnson, your history teacher, is at the board talking about freedom and democracy.

"What are we doing here?" your mind races, not believing your eyes. "Where is the enemy? Who is the enemy? What happened to Tom?" Sitting up, yelling, you cannot see because it's too bright. That voice calls your name, and you search frantically for your weapon, as large figures loom over you. The early morning sun shines in your eyes from an open window. There are lots of different voices.

"Wake up!"

"You're having a bad one. I could hear you down the hall!"

"Are you okay?"

Your sister and parents are standing at your side. You wonder what they are doing in the woods. Then you begin to notice your family surroundings: your model war planes dangle from the ceiling, making eerie shadows on the walls; your plastic soldiers and other war toys stand where you left them before you fell asleep.

You rub your eyes in disbelief. It slowly becomes clear that you've been dreaming. You feel embarrassed.

"He really shouldn't have watched that war movie before he went to bed," your mother says to your father.

Chapter 1

CREATURES OF HABIT

If you are like most kids, you've had nightmares like the one in the opening story. They frighten you. And, like many kids, you may feel even more drawn to war comics, games and movies after a dream like this, as if you need to protect yourself from the enemies in your dreams by reading more about them, or watching them on TV.

At home, your family watches the news, which highlights the conflicts, wars, and violence in our world. You see how this affects your parents. They talk about how badly people treat one another on the job, at the supermarket, on the street, and about the "battles" that go on between neighbors, families and friends.

In school, you pledge your allegiance every day to your country, to serve and defend your nation against "the enemy." You listen to your teachers discuss war. In your history class, you memorize dates of battles that are considered important events. In the schoolyard, you see some kids bullying others, and every day there's at least one fight. After awhile it begins to feel like the "enemy" is everywhere.

Your own life feels like a battle. You don't know how to be, or who you are. You struggle through inner conflicts between the person you are taught you "should" be and the person you feel you are, or want to be. You look for somebody to be like, because you don't really want to be who you see in the mirror.

Once in awhile, you notice some kids at school who don't play with war toys or read war comics. They make a point of treating animals and other living things well, and they are concerned about pollution. They care about people who are old or cannot take care of themselves. Some kids are "vegetarians." They don't eat meat because they don't believe animals ought to be killed for "sport," for food, or for their fur.

Some people make fun of these kids, but you don't think they should be made fun of. You are interested in getting to know them, but you're afraid to admit it because you think people will make fun of you too.

Does any of this sound like you? Do you flare up sometimes without knowing why? Have you got a lot of feelings that are causing you to struggle? You are not alone. This struggle you feel is not unusual.

You probably know that the engine in a car is made up of many parts that work together to create internal combustion. When you flare up from a struggle inside you (your own internal combustion), there's a reason for it. But if you're like most people, you don't always know the reason. The reason is: **your conditioning.**

Conditioning is both the cause of conflict within you and in the world. It is the "war within" and the "war without." In other words, conflict within you is the conflict outside you. It is one and the same thing. In order to understand the conflict between groups of people called war, we must understand the conflict *within* us, our internal battle that is so destructive because we are being pulled apart. On the one hand, we want to be good — but, on the other hand, we are afraid, hurt and angry. We are torn apart, divided and separated in ourselves

and from each other. And all this conflict has its roots in this thing called "conditioning." So, we need to understand what conditioning is, how we get conditioned, what the effects of conditioning are, and how we can be free of it. Let's begin with the question: What is conditioning? And then let's see how conflict created by conditioning within us can cause conflict in the world as war, because there is a definite connection. If we can *understand* this conditioning that creates conflict (inside and outside), we can have peace on earth. Let's start!

What is Conditioning?

You may have heard the word "conditioning" before. To condition means to teach or train. We've all been taught to stop when a traffic light turns red. Have you ever thought about how many times you, as a child, had to be told to stop for a red light before you were actually "conditioned" enough to remember it yourself?

Most of the thoughts in your mind and the actions you take every day are based on how you've been conditioned. You've been conditioned to brush your teeth, to read, to think about yourself in a particular light, and to treat other people in certain ways. We are all creatures of habit who fall into daily routines of walking, talking, thinking and acting.

There are three different kinds of conditioning: biological, physical, and psychological.

1. **Biological conditioning** involves the living processes that are a part of being human and our drive to survive. In order to stay alive, you need food and water. If you go

too long without eating or drinking water, you become hungry and weak. Your body is naturally driven to get what it needs. This conditioning is involuntary — it exists without you having to think about it.

The same goes for your need to sleep. If you've stayed up late or had to get up extremely early, you have experienced how your body feels when it doesn't get enough sleep, and that it's difficult to function well.

2. **Physical conditioning** is training of the body. When you work out in gym class, you get your body in good shape by stretching, bending, reaching, jumping, running, and participating in various sports. After awhile, you perform these physical activities automatically, almost effortlessly, without thinking much about them. Your muscles become *conditioned* to the exercises you put them through. The way you shoot for a basket, or breathe when you run, becomes second nature as your body grows more and more *conditioned* to the workout.

3. **Psychological conditioning** is training of the mind, such as learning to stop for a red light, or brush your teeth. You stop for a red light, or brush your teeth before you go to bed, because you have been *taught* to do so. Behavior that is repeated over and over becomes a "habit." Something you had to think a lot about at first, you now do with hardly any thinking at all.

In our daily lives, we are conditioned by the things we see and the people we know. This conditioning determines how we think, and how we think determines how we act. When you are at home, you are conditioned to think and act the way your family does. At school, your teachers and classmates influence your thoughts and actions. Any activities you participate in outside of home and school can also influence and condition you. Parents and teachers teach you ways to think, act and be because they believe these ways will help you survive.

Not All Conditioning is Positive

You probably know that in the process of conditioning your body to perform positively, training can have negative effects — perhaps causing you to strain a muscle or tear a ligament. The training of your mind can work in the same unexpected way.

If you see a moving car heading straight for you, you are going to move out of the way of that car as fast as you can — without thinking very much before you do. That's an automatic reaction. This is a result of biological conditioning and is lifesaving — and therefore positive.

If, however, you've been pestered by a "bully" at school, and your parents have tried to condition you to fight back, but you don't like to fight and don't believe you should — then you feel an internal struggle called **conflict.** You are in conflict with the bully, you are in conflict with your parents, and you are in conflict with yourself. While the psychological conditioning you received from your family was meant to be positive, in this occasion it is having a negative effect.

This example can also work in reverse: If your parents are nonviolent people who believe you should "turn the other cheek," but you feel you need to fight the bully, you are also in deep conflict, and you may feel great pain inside.

Our conditioning can come from many different directions: from parents, brothers, sisters, teachers, friends, the football team, choir, band, or our religious training. There are times when these different groups have very different ideas about what is "right" or "good" and, as a result, their views may conflict with each other, causing you to feel torn between them.

There is Good News!

The good news is that you can do something about your *psychological* conditioning. While most *biological* conditioning simply is (we are born with it, and it exists no matter what we do), you can have some effect on your mind's conditioning — similar to the way you work on your *physical* conditioning. All it takes is (1) the **interest** to do so, and (2) the **understanding** that you can make a difference.

Perhaps you have the interest and the understanding to do something about your mind's conditioning, but you find it kind of frightening. Fear can stop us in our tracks. Let's begin, then, by talking about fear. I have discovered that when I talk about the things I'm afraid of, I become less afraid. Maybe this will work for you too. Besides, fear is a fascinating part of our conditioning and something *everyone* feels. It is also the cause of a lot of the conflict we feel.

Chapter 2

OUR INSTINCT TO SURVIVE

Fear is the strong feeling we get when we are aware of danger. Because of the violent world in which we live, all of us have felt afraid of something or someone, or many things. Can you remember the last time you were afraid? It doesn't feel good, does it?

Fear is part of our conditioning and something that everyone experiences. You may think that the bully you know never feels afraid, but I can assure you, that bully is just like any other human being. All humans feel fear. Remember when we talked earlier about our biological conditioning being involuntary? Fear is like that. It just appears without our having any say about it. And once it appears, look out! It creates responses that can cause us to totally lose confidence. Here's what happens.

The "Fight or Flight" Response

Have you ever watched a dog and cat when they first meet? They freeze. Then suddenly, either the cat runs away — or, if the dog approaches, the cat may claw the dog. The cat either fights or runs.

We humans do the same thing. Thousands of years ago, primitive humans lived in caves and had to protect themselves from being eaten by wild animals. In those days, they had to fight a wild beast and kill it, or race up a tree to escape being killed. They were forced to be warriors to protect themselves from physical attack. They, too, either fought or ran away. This reaction is known as the **fight or flight** response.

Today, even though we aren't threatened by wild animals very often, deep in our brains we still have a strong "fight or flight" response. I find that amazing. Psychologists, who deal with the workings of the mind and behavior, call this function the "old brain." It seems that this response is passed from one generation to the next, and is common to all humans. Today, our "old brain" continues to tell us to either (1) run away from bullies, or (2) destroy them before they destroy us. We still have strong fears of being physically attacked, and when our "old brain" is sparked, the warrior in us comes out.

Example:

A classmate of yours walks up to you and says, "Hey, Stupid! Give me your money, or I'll change the shape of your nose!"

It can be difficult to ignore a remark like this! What would you do? Would you walk up to your classmate and punch him for saying this (fight)? Or would you run away so you don't have to deal with him (flight)?

Sometimes someone you know can simply call you a name, like "Stupid," or threaten you, and that "old brain" is sparked. Fear pops up and knocks you down before your classmate can. When you feel afraid, you sometimes get caught in the middle of a decision to face the object of your fear, or escape. Sometimes your brain gets so bogged down with the decision that you cannot think or act clearly.

When this happens, have you noticed that your body seems to turn on you? Your heart beats faster, or you sweat. Maybe your hands and feet get cold. (That's where the expression "cold feet" comes from.) These are **physical** responses to being afraid, and most of us are not trained to deal with these physical symptoms of fear. They distract us when we most need to be clear headed and strong minded.

Example:

When Eric, the class bully, spotted me across the playground, my heart skipped a beat. I knew he would antagonize me again. As he walked toward me, my heart began to race, and I began to sweat. My legs felt like they had lead in them, and my feet were too frozen to move. By the time Eric walked up to me, before he even said a word, I was a total wreck.

How we think determines how we act, and when our minds are consumed with fear, our bodies also have an intense fear response.

Fear is also a part of our **psychological** conditioning. We sometimes feel afraid to walk down a dark street, stay home alone at night, or go someplace new for the first time. We are afraid of people who bully us, or people who seem mean or angry. We see situations in our hometowns and across the globe that cause us to feel fear. We fear burglars, killers, drug addicts and mentally deranged people. Fear is a part of the way we think and respond in our everyday lives.

Example:

Your parents have instructed you never to open the door to a stranger. Someone rings your doorbell one day, saying, "My keys are locked in my car. Can I use your phone to call for help?"

What do you do? These kinds of situations put us into conflict. We have a fear of strangers, combined with a desire to help those in distress.

Sometimes fear causes us to say things we don't intend to say, and act in ways that we would normally not act. Some of us tend to come on strong and react violently in the face of fear (fight); others back off or hide (flight). Both reactions to fear put us into immediate conflict, either with another person or with ourselves. Fear is a major component of the invisible enemy (conditioning) and a major cause of conflict.

One of the ways to learn to handle fear is to really look at it to understand what it does to you. Think of a situation that frightens you, and let's try to understand it.

Things That Make Me Afraid

1. A situation that makes me feel fear is:

_____ .

2. When I feel afraid, my body:

_____ .

3. When I feel afraid, I think:

_____.

4. As a result, the way I act is:

_____.

There is no "right" or "wrong" to the way you act when you feel afraid. How you act is based on (1) your biological conditioning, which happens spontaneously without your controlling it, and (2) your psychological conditioning, which is how you've been taught to act. The way you are conditioned to think and act is the only behavior you know.

There is another aspect to survival that we need to look at. Every human being needs to survive physically, which means that each of us requires adequate food, shelter and clothing. Without these necessities, we would perish. So, we have an instinct towards **physical survival**.

There is another human drive, which comes out of our conditioning: the drive for **psychological survival**. This is rooted in the "me" wanting to survive at all costs, to win out over the "other." And sometimes this "me" becomes "we," an association of like-minded "me/s" who have banded together into some sort of group, tribe, religion or nation, who then must survive against other groups, tribes, religions, or nations. You can see how this can lead to war.

If we are to understand "conditioning," we need to understand the difference between physical survival (which is necessary) and this primitive drive for psychological survival

23

(which is unnecessary). *The drive for psychological survival can be dangerous and detrimental to our physical survival.*

We are conditioned to think in terms of "*me* first!" Conditioning creates the "me" who is the most important one, and creates conflict between all the "me/s" or "we/s," and the "they/s!" This may sound complicated, but it is really quite simple. When we are selfish, placing ourselves or our group or nation over others, then we are creating division and conflict. As we begin to understand conditioning, we begin to understand how we reinforce the divisions between us.

In the pages that follow, you will have the opportunity to look at your conditioning to see how it causes you conflict. Once you become aware of the behavior that puts you into conflict, you can change it if you want to. I don't know about you, but for me, knowing that I have the power to change my behavior is very exciting.

Chapter 3

THE ONLY BEHAVIOR WE KNOW

What is Conflict?

To be in conflict means to struggle, battle, make war. To be in conflict is to oppose someone or something and to feel the pain of that opposition, physically and mentally. You can tell when you are in conflict. You feel caught between two opposing forces. You're scared to take action, and scared not to take action. This leaves you feeling pretty helpless.

If, for example, you want to attend a party and your parents don't think you should go, you and your parents are in conflict. This is conflict between you and *other people*. The situation we described earlier, in which a person wants to use your telephone to get help, is an example of conflict between two opposing thoughts in *your own mind:* wanting to help someone and being concerned about opening the door to a stranger. In either situation, if you can resolve the conflict so that both "sides" are somehow satisfied, there will be no "war."

You're probably thinking, "No way!" There's no way to resolve a conflict in which I want to go to a party and my parents say no. There's no way to help the driver of the stalled car and also respect my parents' wishes. The truth is, there is. And I think you will agree with me after you've read further.

Some people believe that a certain type of conflict is good because it teaches you how to work through problems and strengthens your ability to resolve them. That's true. Math problems are very good for developing our brains. But other kinds of conflict are harmful and sometimes cause unnecessary pain and hurt. Some conflicts develop into wars — either personal wars between two or more people, or international wars between countries.

Perhaps you've never thought that it was possible to resolve all of your conflicts. Maybe you've always thought that there is no way out of certain conflicts, and that you just have to live with them. If you think about it, any war begins as a disagreement between two or more people; if those people can resolve their disagreement, a war can be prevented. Perhaps if you and I learn to resolve the little wars in ourselves and between us, we'll know how to participate in resolving the major ones that plague our country and others all over the world. What do you think?

Conflict is a Symptom of Fear

As I said earlier, when you find yourself in a situation that causes you to feel fear, you make a decision to either fight or run away. However, the decision to fight puts you into instant conflict with another person:

> "I have to teach this idiot a thing or two!"
> "I hate this guy!"
> "I'll show him!"

And the decision to run away puts you into instant conflict with yourself. You think thoughts that don't make you feel very good, such as those on the next page:

26

"I can't fight him; I'm not strong enough!"
"I hate running away, but if I don't, I'll get beaten up!"
"I wish I were like Rambo!"

You and I have been conditioned to believe that conflict is a natural and necessary part of the life we live. However, with an *interest* in *understanding* conflict, and how conditioning causes conflict, you and I can prevent it.

Assuming that you are interested in gaining this understanding, let's take a look at conflict — and learn to be more aware of when we are experiencing it.

Tracing Symptoms to Causes

You know that when you have a bad cold, you are miserable. You are aware that you have a cold because you sneeze, cough, feel tired or run a fever. These are *symptoms* of your cold.

But do you know where the cold began — in other words, the cause of the cold? Maybe you didn't wear enough warm clothing on a cold day. Maybe you didn't take care of yourself, eat right or sleep enough. Perhaps you let yourself get run down.

You can treat your cold with remedies to reduce the symptoms of sneezing and coughing — to "fix" your cold. But if you want to prevent getting a cold again, you need to examine the possible causes and avoid them. How can you prevent getting a cold? On the following page, write down three steps you might take...

1. _____ .

2. _____ .

3. _____ .

Keep in mind that these are steps to *avoid* a cold. It could be that your cold was *caused* by your not taking these steps.

In order to take steps
not to catch a cold again,
it's necessary to understand why
you got a cold in the first place.

In order to better understand conditioning, we can also trace backwards — from symptoms to cause, just like we did with the cold. If you have a disagreement with someone you know, you can find ways to work out your differences — to "fix" your relationship. But in order to *prevent* future disagreements, you must understand how your conflict *began* in the first place. The *symptoms* may be fighting, yelling, disagreeing, and the temporary solution may be to simply stop fighting. But once you figure out what *caused* the fight, you can then understand how to prevent another fight from occurring.

In order not to fight again,
you have to understand why
you started fighting in the first place.

Let's look at the following examples and think about how these conflicts come about.

Example #1:

My father asked me to mow the lawn. I was angry with him, and I refused.

Symptom of conflict:

I mow the lawn every weekend, but this time I refused.

Possible causes of conflict:

1. I was angry with my father for not allowing me to go to the party.
2. I was trying to get back at my father.
3. I didn't tell Dad I was angry; I kept it inside, and it came out this way.

Example #2:

Jurors in a court of law have to either convict or release attackers who chased a man through a neighborhood at night, and seriously injured him using clubs. Because the man's skin was a different color than theirs, the attackers felt he didn't "belong" in that neighborhood — even though his car had broken down.

Symptom of conflict:

Several attackers were beating up another human being.

Possible causes of conflict:

1. Some people are conditioned to believe that any "outsider" who wanders through a neighborhood late at night, far from where the "outsider" lives, is suspicious and should be challenged, and possibly attacked.
2. Some people think that an "outsider" will lie about his car breaking down in order to cover up his real intentions, and he should not be believed.
3. Some people are conditioned to be suspicious of people who have a different skin color.

Once we understand what causes our conflict, we are better equipped to prevent it from recurring. If we don't understand the cause, we don't really understand the situation, and the fighting and anger are likely to come back again and again.

Let's see what you've come to understand about the two previous examples.

1. In Example #1, I think the son could prevent a future argument with his father by:

_____ .

2. In Example #2, I think people in that neighborhood could prevent future beatings of innocent persons by:

_____ .

You have choices in dealing with any situation that causes you conflict.

You can:

1. Look at the **symptoms** and find a "quick fix" solution;

-AND/OR-

2. Look at the **cause** and find a way to prevent the problem from happening again.

People in conflict usually feel hurt or angry. Not knowing any other way to handle their feelings, they sometimes take their hurt or anger out on another person. On a larger scale, this is how we get into wars.

We become afraid. We fight or run away.
Fighting or running put us in conflict.
Inner conflict causes outer conflict.
Outer conflict causes war.

Perhaps if you take a closer look at those times you've been in conflict, you can better understand what was going on inside you. Let's take a look at both "fight" and "flight" reactions.

A. The "Fight" Reaction

Can you see how a "fight" reaction can cause conflict? Think of the last time you witnessed a fight or took part in one. This could be a physical or verbal fight.

1. The last time I saw or participated in a (physical or verbal) "fight" reaction was:

2. The kind of conflict that arose from this "fight" reaction was:

_____ .

3. The outcome of this "fight" reaction was:

_____ .

4. What fighting did was:

     (a) Create conflict
     (b) Correct the conflict
     (c) Increase the conflict
     (d) Make everything better

B. The "Flight Reaction"

Can you see how a "flight" reaction can cause conflict? Think of the last time you ran away — or saw someone else run away — from a physical or verbal fight.

1. The last time I saw or participated in a "flight" reaction was:

_____ .

2. The kind of conflict that arose from this "flight" reaction was:

_____ .

3. The outcome of this "flight" reaction was:

_____ .

4. What running away did was:
    (a) Create conflict
    (b) Correct the conflict
    (c) Increase the conflict
    (d) Make everything better

Sometimes we decide to stay and face the action that causes us conflict, and sometimes we decide to run away from it. Neither reaction is "right" or "wrong." We all make such a decision based on our drive to survive. It's helpful, however, to look at how you react to gain an understanding of what makes you react the way you do.

C. The Decision I Made

The last time I was in conflict with someone,

1. I made the decision to *run away* from or *leave* the conflict, because:

_____ .

When I ran away, I felt:

_____ .

33

2. I made the decision to *fight* or *argue* because:

_____ .

When I finished fighting, I felt:

_____ .

So now you know that conflict comes from being conditioned to act in a certain way, but feeling that you would rather act in a different way.

We can feel conflict in a small situation:

"I want to shout at Eric for making fun of me, but I've been conditioned to believe that shouting isn't nice."

Or we can feel conflict on a grand scale:

"I don't want to carry a weapon and fight in a war, especially against the country of my family's origin."

The Causes of Conflict

We said earlier that the way to gain understanding is to examine causes. The causes of conflict we feel in any situation are (1) how we think, (2) how we act, and (3) the effect of our thoughts on our actions.

1. **How we think.** If I think my father is mean when he doesn't let me go to a party, perhaps I am conditioned to

think that my parents are "mean" when they don't let me do what I want to do.

2. **How we act.** I became angry with my father and wouldn't mow the lawn. It might be that I am conditioned to act hostilely toward someone I believe has been hostile to me.

3. **The effect of our thoughts on our actions.** Since I thought my father was acting in a "mean" way, I reacted by being "mean" too. Because I've been conditioned to believe that not letting me have my way is being "mean," and because I've been conditioned to "fight fire with fire," I created conflict by my behavior toward my father.

The way you think and the way you act are dependent upon how you've been conditioned. Therefore, any conflict you feel (at school, at home, in the outside world) can be traced back to your conditioning.

1. The thought in my mind at the time I made the decision to (fight) (run away) was:

_____.

2. Based on that thought, the action I took at that time, was:

_____.

35

3. My thoughts and actions are based on my conditioning. The conditioning that affected my behavior at that time was:

_____ .

Would you be interested if I told you that I have a way for you to begin to change your conditioning and deal with your fears? In the pages that follow, you will discover some steps you can take to feel more secure about yourself. You will also discover how you became conditioned in the first place. This awareness will bring you closer to an understanding of conflict, and what you can do about it.

The Boy Who Thought He Could Fly
A Story

"Faster than a speeding bullet, able to leap tall buildings in a single bound. Look, it's a bird! It's a plane! It's Superman!"

Billy had just finished watching the video "Superman" and his favorite regular TV show, "Superboy," was now on. He watched the image of his caped hero leaping tall buildings. He draped a towel over his own shoulders to feel like Superboy as his eyes took in the images of human beings performing superhuman feats.

When the show ended, the boy stretched and yawned. He turned toward the stairs of his house and climbed to the third story. He walked over to the only window and opened it. Expressionless, he looked down the many feet to the ground below, and then climbed onto the window ledge. It was a

glorious summer evening, and he felt a rush of energy pulse through his small body. He felt powerful.

Billy's mother was downstairs in the kitchen washing dishes. Her husband was in town doing errands, and she was thinking of what to make for dinner. She heard the sound of the TV and felt assured that her son was safely involved in his favorite show. As she washed dishes before the kitchen window, there was a sudden movement — as if a large bird had dropped from the sky, swooping down to the ground. There was a loud thump and a small human cry.

Shocked for a moment, the mother stood frozen with water running over her hands, thinking "Bird? Or boy?" Terror gripped her heart as she raced outside to find her son lying on the ground, the Superboy towel-cape draped over his still body. Miraculously, he groaned and began to move. Incredibly, Billy was not hurt. He had fallen three stories and didn't have a scratch. "I did it, just like Superboy!" the young boy exclaimed.

Billy's parents were thankful and amazed that their son was alright, but they were disturbed because he did not seem to understand the danger in what he had done and how lucky he had been. Because he had been unhurt, they were afraid he might try it again and really hurt himself.

To convince him of the danger, the boy's father went up to the third story and pushed a large watermelon out. The melon fell heavily through the air and landed with a shattering thud in a mass of squashed pieces.

Chapter 4

THE THINGS WE ARE TRAINED
TO BELIEVE

The reason I told you the "Superboy" story, based on a real event, is that I've heard and read a lot about young people imitating what they see on TV and in the movies. Although this boy was lucky, most of what I read or hear has a tragic ending. For a very young person, there is sometimes difficulty in telling the difference between fantasy and reality. This young boy who jumped out the window is an example. For a few moments, he was psychologically conditioned to believe that he could fly. Of course, he couldn't and he was very lucky to survive the jump.

How We are Conditioned

We have been talking about different kinds of conditioning, but our main focus has been on psychological conditioning, because that is the primary reason for conflict in our lives. We can't see the conditioning in our minds, so it's important to talk about it and become more aware of its presence.

Rules and Regulations

We discussed earlier how parents and teachers condition us to think and act in certain ways, because they believe these ways will help us survive in the world. At times, adults also condition us in order to help *them* survive. For example, if your parents want you home by, say, 9:00 p.m., one reason may be that you must get up early the next morning. Another reason could be that then they'll be able to sleep well in preparation for work the next day.

While getting home in time is important in maintaining harmony within your family, following certain rules and regulations can also condition us in negative ways. An extreme example: When thousands of German people became Nazis and followed Hitler's rules and regulations in the early 1940s, and tortured millions of Jews (people who did not fit Hitler's image of what people should be like), the world suffered one of the worst tragedies in history.

We find, as we live and work in the world, that there are many people who would have us live by their rules and regulations — to make life easier for them. Therefore, we are conditioned to behave in a certain way — for them, and not necessarily for our best interest. This kind of conditioning can cause deep conflict.

Reward and Punishment

If you have a dog at home, are you aware that when you teach your dog to beg, roll over, or do other tricks, that you are "conditioning" your dog? When you teach your dog a trick, you normally offer a biscuit or some other treat when your dog has performed well. On the other hand, if your dog has wet the floor, or chewed up your shoes, you scold your dog to prevent that kind of thing from happening again. You condition your dog not to "misbehave." This system is one of reward and punishment. You reward your dog for a trick well done, and punish your dog for behaving badly.

When we want *people* to act in a certain way, we also reward or punish them. We offer love, or take our love away. We treat them well, or become angry with them.

As you were growing up, your family rewarded you for the tiniest things — saying "Mommy" or "Daddy," for example. Perhaps they smiled and hugged you. The smile and hug were your reward. If you spilled milk or touched something breakable, they may have shouted, "No!" in an angry voice. This was punishment for doing something "wrong." Punishment can also be the taking away of something — such as refusing to talk to you, or not allowing you to go to a party.

1. When was the last time that someone used punishment to get you to do something for them? Describe the situation:

_____

_____ .

2. Have you ever used punishment to get someone to do something for you? If so, what happened?

_____

_____

_____ .

3. Has someone rewarded you to get you to do something for them? If so, what were the circumstances?

_____

_____ .

4. Can you think of a time when you rewarded someone for doing something for you? What was the reward?

_____

_____ .

Conditioned by Our Surroundings

As we're growing up, we spend most of our lives in family surroundings that condition us psychologically and determine how we think and act. Habits, traditions, customs, values and beliefs are some of the things we "pick up" from our families that determine our behavior.

1. **Habits:** A habit is a manner of behavior that we learn and repeat so often that it becomes second nature.

Example:

Lois has a habit of smiling every time she is hurt, so nobody will know she feels sad.

2. **Traditions:** A tradition is a belief or practice handed down by word of mouth or by example from one generation to another.

Example:

It is a tradition in Solomon's family to light eight candles for the celebration of Hanukkah, a Jewish holiday. It is a tradition in Karen's family to buy a fir tree at Christmas time and decorate it with ornaments made by the family.

3. **Customs:** A custom is a long established practice which people treat as an unwritten law.

Example:

It is a custom in Jan's family to offer any visitor a place to sleep for the night. It is a custom in Marc's family to say a prayer before eating the evening meal.

4. **Values:** Value is the worth or importance that people attach to other people or things.

Example:

Having lots of money is very important to Steve. Manuel believes that doing well in school is a top priority.

5. **Beliefs:** A belief is a state of mind in which trust is placed in some person or idea.

Example:

Marilyn has a strong belief that people who devote themselves to God and being good will go to Heaven when they die.

Understanding How We Create Differences Between People

Habits, traditions, customs, values and beliefs make up our psychological conditioning. For example, you may learn as you grow up that you must attend church every week; otherwise, you are not a "good" person. This may be a family or cultural belief passed down from generation to generation. Going to church every week is a *custom* that has become a *habit*, and a *tradition*. You are, therefore, conditioned to believe that if you don't go to church, you are "bad."

One day you meet Susan. Susan does not go to church. You don't know why she doesn't, but you come to the instantaneous conclusion that Susan is bad because she does not attend church. Perhaps other people in your community have talked about this and are also suspicious of her. You and others are *conditioned* to believe that any "good" person would attend church.

Let's consider why Susan might not attend Church. Perhaps her family doesn't believe in traditional religious practice. Or perhaps she has spiritual beliefs that do not include going to a church. Perhaps her customs, habits and traditions are not the same as yours.

The important thing to see is that by making Susan "different" in your mind, she has become threatening and you have created conflict between you and her.

When I create a difference between myself and another person, I'm creating a separation that divides us.

Imagine yourself looking at Susan in a new way. When you find out that Susan does not go to church, you become interested in knowing why. The fact that she is different from you makes you curious about her. You decide that the next time you see her, you will ask her why you haven't seen her in church and if she ever goes to church. You will ask out of interest, rather than in a way that accuses her of doing something wrong.

Imagine yourself listening to Susan's answers to your questions. How do her answers make you feel? Do you compare her way of life to yours? Do you think you are better than she is? Does she show you something about your way of life that helps you to understand your conditioning?

Keep in mind, when you meet someone different from you:

This person is presenting me with a wonderful opportunity to learn how I may be creating conflict in my relationships.

Take a moment to consider this statement:

**"No one is either an angel or a devil,
a cowboy or an Indian,
a good guy or a bad guy!"**

Chapter 5

HOW DO WE KNOW WHAT'S REAL?

Remember the boy in the story who jumped from the third story? Do you know what caused him to believe that he could fly? It was psychological conditioning. He saw Superman and Superboy do it and, for a few moments, *believed* he could too.

Mind Tricks

These days, movies are very realistic. It appears that someone is really flying, or that someone is really getting shot. Filmmakers create illusions for our believing eyes. If you saw the movie "E.T.," you saw a realistic make-believe creature from outer space and young boys riding their bicycles through the air, over the moon. It was thrilling to watch. This was such a wonderful fantasy that we wanted to believe it was true, even though we knew it wasn't. Filmmakers are like magicians: their hands are quicker than our eyes. Some examples of illusion are illustrated on the next two pages to show you that *what you think you see is not always what's really there.*

The Effects of Violent Movies

Most of us know that the violence in movies and on TV is only pretend. Those people on the screen are not really hurting or killing each other, they are acting. However, the makers of films create tricks to make it appear to our minds that the

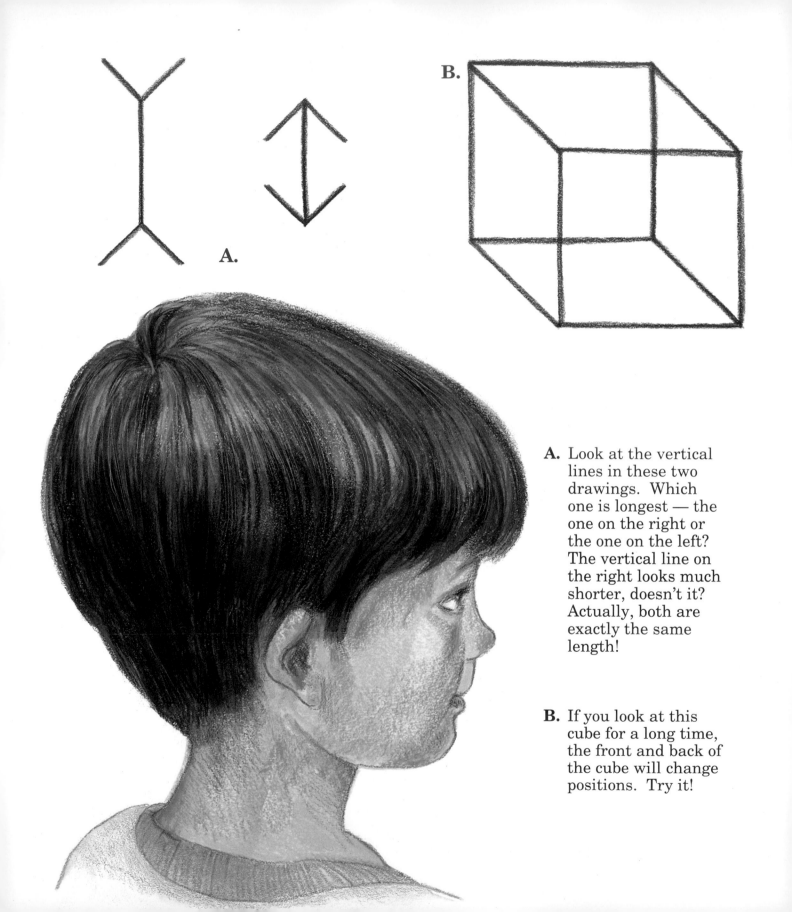

A. Look at the vertical lines in these two drawings. Which one is longest — the one on the right or the one on the left? The vertical line on the right looks much shorter, doesn't it? Actually, both are exactly the same length!

B. If you look at this cube for a long time, the front and back of the cube will change positions. Try it!

C. Do you see an arrow with a cross, or do you see angry faces?

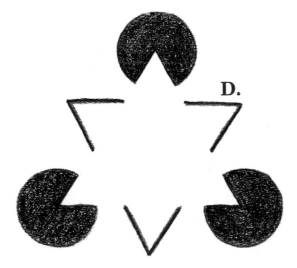

D. Do you see two triangles in this picture? There aren't actually any triangles! Your mind is filling in the blanks.

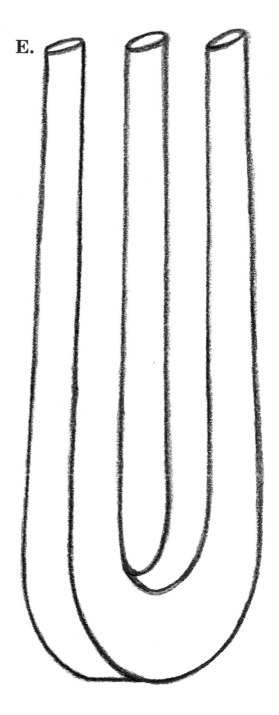

E. Do you see why this drawing is called "the impossible magnet"?

action is real. But because the action is not real, filmmakers feel that violent movies will not have a lasting or harmful effect on us.

I disagree. I think that violent movies can harm us in many ways, and one way is that they *condition* us to believe that there are "good guys" and "bad guys" in this world — and that it's either/or.

Remember when we discussed the two biologically conditioned reactions to fear? One is to get violent (fight), and the other is to run and hide out of fear (flight). The "bad guys" in movies make us feel we must either fight or run away, and the "good guys" or "heroes" represent those people who will save us. We are left with the impression that there are two kinds of people in this world: (1) people we must fight or flee from, and (2) people who rescue us. So, we are conditioned to fight, run away, or be rescued. It is unfortunate that none of these impressions help us learn how to take care of ourselves, or how to resolve conflict.

Heroes and Villains

A hero or heroine is admired for his or her achievements and qualities, someone who shows great courage and strength of character. For example, firemen have been trained (conditioned) to enter burning buildings to save people who may be trapped inside. A fireman who does this is a definite hero in my book.

Every so often, we will hear about a man or woman who has truly performed an act of courage to save another life, or to stand up for what he or she believes. Martin Luther King, Jr.

actively worked for equality for black people, even though he knew that this put him personally at risk. A person who believes something so strongly that he or she will put their own life on the line for the benefit of others can also be a hero.

When I was a young boy, I read comic books and my favorites were those with "super heroes." I read about Superman, Batman and Captain Marvel. I also read war stories and watched a lot of "cowboy and Indian" movies. Over the years, our heroes have changed. If you've been watching television, you've seen many programs in which there are heroes ("good" guys), and villains ("bad" guys). But some of the so-called "heroes" act just as violently as the "villains" do.

In these movies, we watch adults whom we admire act violently. We think to ourselves: If adults do it, it must be okay. We are influenced by the behavior we're watching, and are encouraged to imitate it. Therefore, we are *conditioned* to be violent; we are taught that violence is something good guys do too. Some of these heroes use fists, knives or guns to fight the "bad" guys — the same weapons the "bad" guys use. They fight fire with fire, violence with more violence. Violence becomes not only acceptable, but praiseworthy. And we become more and more conditioned to accept violence and admire it. This creates the confusion that a hero is not a peaceful person, but a violent one.

As a result, by watching these movies, we learn to be violent. We imitate what we see on TV. Remember the young boy who jumped out of the window to imitate Superboy? If this same boy had watched cowboys shooting guns on television and had access to a gun in his home, do you see the possibility that

he might use the gun and hurt or kill someone? Accidents like this happen all too often.

The more violence we watch, the more we accept it as a natural part of our daily lives. That's what conditioning is: it's training, repeated over and over again. We have been conditioned to believe that a hero *fights* for us. Is that the kind of hero you see on TV? But does it make sense to say that in order to have peace, we must fight for it? Or, does it make more sense to say: In order to have peace, we must make peace?

Exercise:

A. Name three people you think of as heroes:

1. _____ .

2. _____ .

3. _____ .

B. Why are these people heroes to you?

_____

_____ .

C. Are you conditioned to believe that a hero is violent, or do you think that a hero is peaceful?

_____ .

D. Have you ever wanted to be a hero?

_____ .

E. What kind of hero would you like to be?

_____ .

F. What would being a "hero" do for you?

_____

_____ .

G. Do you think that acting like a hero can create conflict
   inside you — between what you actually are and what
   you (and others) think you should be?

_____

_____ .

Chapter 6

SEEING THROUGH OUR CONDITIONING

Now you know that you are conditioned by family, school, friends and other people that you see every day. You are conditioned by customs, values, beliefs, traditions and habits, and you are influenced by movies you see in theaters and on television.

You know that the ways in which you have been conditioned are not necessarily "right" or "wrong." But you are also aware that your conditioning can cause conflict.

Your next question might be: If no way is "right" and no way is "wrong," how do I resolve conflict? I suggest that you:

1. Think through each conflict;
2. Look at the causes of your conditioned thinking;
3. Take time to understand why people are divided in their differences.

Yes, this will take time and energy, but it gets to the core of the matter, rather than labeling other people "right," "wrong," "good" or "bad." Doesn't it make more sense to take a path that will lead to truth — peacefully?

Exercise:

On the following page are some examples of conditioned reactions...

A. I've been treating a kid at school badly. I'm not sure why; I've just always treated him that way.

B. Every time my mother asks me to help around the house, I grumble and complain.

C. Whenever a teacher calls on me in class, I clam up and can't say anything. I get so tense that I can't even think whether or not I know the answer to the question.

D. One of my classmates calls me names. I always respond by calling him a name back.

Select a conditioned reaction that you have engaged in lately. Use one of the above examples as a starting point, or think of your own.

1. My conditioned reaction was:

   _____.

2. What brought this reaction about was:

   _____.

3. The causes of this conditioned reaction were:

   _____

   _____.

4. What the other person(s) in this situation said that may have caused my conditioned reaction:

_____ .

5. What I said that may have caused a conditioned reaction in the other person:

_____ .

Exercise:

List some ways in which you are divided from others by your beliefs:

He/She/They Believe:

A. _____ .

B. _____ .

C. _____ .

However, I/We Believe:

A. _____ .

B. _____ .

C. _____ .

If you want to go to a party and your father doesn't want you to go, you are in conflict. You see yourself as the "good" guy and your father as the "bad" guy. Your father may see himself as the "good" guy and you as the "bad" guy. When we look only at what I/We believe, and call ourselves "the good guys," then we are calling He/She/Them (anybody who does not agree with us) "the bad guys." As soon as we set up a situation like this in which we believe we are good or right, and "they" are bad or wrong, we have created conflict.

Have you created conflict recently by seeing someone as the "bad guy" and yourself as the "good guy"? Perhaps you had a disagreement with your parent, brother, sister, classmate, teacher. Name two ways you set up the situation of "good guy" versus "bad guy":

1. _____ .

2. _____ .

Each person sees things from his or her own perspective. Nobody is right and nobody is wrong in these situations. Have you ever looked through a glass prism? From one angle you see blue; from another angle you see red, or yellow. That's how it is looking at "truth." What you see depends on where you're standing. We grow up in different families, in different countries, and we speak different languages, so we have various perspectives on what life is all about. And this can create conflict, in ourselves and in the world.

Beyond our differences, however, there is a truth that is real for most people. While we may have different approaches, one of the ways we are the same is that most human beings want love and peace in their lives. It seems strange to me that we have accepted the idea that we must *fight* to get it!

Images That Condition Us

Statistics show that the average kid watches between 30 and 50 hours of TV every week. So, the average kid watches 30,000 to 40,000 commercials each year! Do you watch that much? If you do, by the time you reach your 18th birthday, you will have sat in front of the television for approximately 25,000 hours. That's a lot of TV. If how we spend our time affects who we are and what we do, then watching that much television has a significant effect on us.

There are, of course, quite a few creative, informative, entertaining and relaxing programs on television. The important thing is to (1) watch TV selectively and intelligently, and (2) understand how you are influenced by its powerful effects.

Statistics also reveal that if you watch 25,000 hours of TV, by the time you reach the age of 18 you will have watched over 25,000 murders. Remember when we discussed how repeated behavior conditions us to act and respond in certain ways? Someone who has watched 25,000 murders on television is more likely to be conditioned to believe that:

1. The world is made up of heroes and villains;
2. Murders are everyday occurrences we must live with.
3. If we're going to survive, we have to either fight or run.

How many of the statements (at the end of page 59) do you believe? If you believe those statements are true, it's time to take a look at your conditioning.

I Will Fight No More, Forever
A Story

Some of the effects of conditioning seem harmless, or even beneficial. But are we aware of the destructive effects of conditioning on our lives and in the world? There are numerous wars and personal tragedies that have taken the effects of conditioning to the most disastrous conclusions. One of the saddest situations involved American Indians and European settlers in America.

When Europeans landed in what is now referred to as the United States of America, about 1,000,000 Indians were living in this country. The Indians had a very developed culture and lifestyle in harmony with the land. However, Europeans considered Indians to be savages. By 1900, the effects of new diseases and strong liquor (which arrived with the white people) and 300 years of warfare had reduced this number to 237,000. That is a loss of over 750,000 human beings.

The early history of the United States includes a string of battles between the settlers and Indians, from the Massacre of 1622 and the French and Indian War, to Pontiac's Rebellion, the Battle of Tippecanoe, the Sioux War, the Nez Perce War, and the final terrible Battle of Wounded Knee Creek.

There are those who believe that white men were heroic in conquering the Indians. As I see it, Europeans did not "win the West" with heroism. It was won by one set of human beings killing and taking land from another set of human beings, using force, guns and violence. Even though I played "cowboys and Indians" as a small boy and always wanted to be a cowboy because I thought they were the good guys, as an adult I see it differently. Had white men and Indians found a way to share the land, that truly would have been heroic.

White men were victorious over the Indians because they killed them, overtook their land, and drove them onto "reservations" — land that "white men" designated for Indians only. How would you react if thousands of people came to the United States and tried to take the land, driving the existing inhabitants — including your family — onto reservations?

The following quote is from the well-known Nez Perce Indian Chief, Joseph, about the battle he was forced to fight with the U.S. Army as he tried to lead his people across Montana and Idaho into Canada:

"I am tired of fighting. Our chiefs are killed... the old men are all killed.... It is cold and we have no blankets. The little children are freezing to death. My people, some of them, have run away to the hills and have no blankets, no food; no one knows where they are, perhaps freezing to death. I want time to look for my children and see how many of them I can find. Maybe I shall find them among the dead. Hear me, my chiefs, I am tired; my heart is sick and sad. From where the sun now stands, I will fight no more, forever."

Chapter 7

WAR HAS BECOME A TRADITION

The history of man is filled with war. For centuries we have attempted to solve violence with more violence. From the first North American colonial establishments in the early 1600s through the 1900s, there have been literally hundreds of wars. This form of dealing with conflict has been handed down generation after generation. As you've already learned, a tradition is something we have grown so accustomed to that it becomes part of our natural way of life. War has become a tradition.

As I grew up, I began to see that the "good guys" and "bad guys" were not good or bad. In the case of North America, there were simply two different cultures of people, one already living on the land, and one desiring to live on the land. That they could not live on the land together, in peace, is the sad story. Although there certainly were white people and Indians who got along together, we never hear much about them. The most publicized point of view is that the Indians were savages and that the land had to be taken from them.

This violent attitude is not just an American one, and it did not begin with the Europeans who came over to the United States as pilgrims. For as far back as historical records go, there are tales of violence and methods of dealing with it that are just as violent. It seems our "old brains," the ones that have been with us since the days of the cave man, have had us fighting or fleeing for thousands of years.

In spite of the fact that there have been many attempts to make us more peaceful, we have remained a conditioned-to-be-violent world. When you consider that white men won the West with a Winchester repeating rifle that shot rapid-fire bullets and slaughtered Indians by the hundreds, while the Indians protected their people with bows and arrows, or single-shot rifles, you might ask, "How could human beings do that to other human beings?" However, compare this to TV programs and news events of today, and you begin to feel that human beings have not changed much over the centuries.

Exercise:

Have you ever played "cowboys and Indians"? If you have, you've played for fun. Let's play it now in a different way. As you play, be aware of how it makes you feel to be a cowboy or an Indian. Imagine that you are fighting for real and that your life is at stake.

1. Divide yourselves into cowboys and Indians. Pretend that cowboys have just arrived on Indian territory. The cowboys announce that the land is theirs. The Indians claim that the land has been Indian territory for as long as they can remember.

   A. The head cowboy says:

   _____

   _____ .

B. The Indian chief responds:

_____

_____ .

C. Keep the dialogue going between the cowboy and Indian chief for about two minutes. Fight out your differences until somebody "wins" or "loses."

2. How did it feel to be a cowboy or an Indian?

A. Did you feel superior or inferior? Why?

_____ .

B. Did you like your "role" as cowboy or Indian? Why?

_____ .

C. What did you think of the "other side" when you were fighting?

_____ .

3. Did you do anything in the game that made you feel heroic?

_____

_____ .

4. What are the differences between cowboys and Indians?

_____

_____ .

5. How do you think the differences might be resolved?

_____

_____ .

6. How are cowboys and Indians the same?

_____

_____ .

You can probably see how your thinking as a cowboy or Indian influenced your actions. The actions you took certainly influenced the thoughts and actions of the person to whom your actions were directed. Imagine! All the actions we take begin in our brain, which is a center of great activity — especially when we are in conflict. In the next chapter, we will take a look at our brain to see how it works in conflict situations.

Chapter 8

OUR BRAIN IS LIKE A COMPUTER

The human brain is a complex and wonderful machine. It is the source of our thoughts, feelings and actions. In this chapter, I will show you how your brain can also create conflict. Once you see how your brain does this, you will be able to learn to stop it as it is happening — just by being AWARE.

The brain stores all kinds of information and can recall millions of bits of knowledge to help you live. You remember how to get home after school. You recognize your family, your house, your family car, your dog, your cat, your clothes. If you want to write a letter, your brain cues your hand to pick up a pen and use it. That's all thanks to your memory. Imagine, for a moment, that the information coming into your brain is stored as if on tape by a movie recorder. And your view of the world, formed out of this recorded information, is projected onto the outside world, as if by a movie projector onto a movie screen. When you need certain information, your brain, functioning like a computer, calls it up from where it is stored in memory.

Leaving Room for Human Error

Sometimes even the finest computer makes a mistake. The reason is usually that it has been fed incorrect information. If you've worked on a computer, you know that sometimes you can enter a word or other information that is not exactly correct and produce unexpected results. So it is with the brain. Remember the boy who watched "Superboy" and jumped out of the third story window because he thought he could fly? The information that entered his brain about humans flying was incorrect. He confused fantasy with reality while watching a television program.

There are many different ways our brains can take in incorrect information, and sometimes we don't find out that it's incorrect for a long time. Other times we get so used to the information, that even when we find out it's incorrect, we have a hard time correcting it. The following examples show how this can affect our lives:

Elana's Conditioning

When Elana bought herself something new, her sister, who was usually kind to her, would shout at her and accuse her of being selfish for not buying her one too. Because her sister repeatedly acted in this way, Elana began to believe that before doing something for herself, she had to make other people happy. She also believed that anyone who was kind might really be a bully in disguise.

When Elana grew up and became a designer, she worked for an employer who admired her designs and was kind to her. Elana was suspicious that her employer would blow up at her one day; as a result, she remained cool toward her employer, never trusting the encouragement she was given.

Questions:

1. Can you see a correlation between Elana's experience with her sister and her relationship with her employer?

   _____.

2. Do you think her early experience may have conditioned her to act in a certain way now?

   _____.

3. How do you think she was conditioned to believe that outwardly "kind" people might be bullies in disguise?

   _____

   _____.

4. Can you see how Elana's conditioning to be wary of those who are nice to her could lead to major problems in her life?

   _____.

Ted's Conditioning

Ted believed that if he didn't bully someone every now and then, that he would wind up getting bullied. Ted's father used to bully him a lot, but Ted discovered that if he got angry with his father, his father bullied him less.

When Ted grew up, he became a politician. He became known for his bullying tactics and believed that in dealing with other countries, the United States ought to show its power. He believed that if we don't control "them," "they" will control us.

Questions:

1. How was Ted conditioned in his early life?

_____ .

2. What effect did his conditioning have on his later life?

_____ .

3. Can you see how Ted's individual conditioning wound up having a global effect?

_____ .

If we have been conditioned to think that Russians are warlike, or that white people are superior to black people, or that Indians are not smart, it may take time to correct this information because the images we hold can be very strong. It takes careful attention and awareness to change our thinking and way we see the world. It's important, therefore, to become conscious of our thoughts — about others as well as about ourselves.

Although it doesn't intend to, our brain sometimes creates conflict. The information we feed our body computer may be incomplete, or the way we sort out the information may be incorrect. Let's take a look at some of the things that can happen as a result.

Self-Consciousness: How We See Ourselves

If you've ever been to a party where you were self-conscious because you didn't know anyone, or because you felt your clothes were out of place, you know that self-consciousness is being acutely aware of how you think other people see you.

People in your life may say, for example, "You're too shy," or "You're so noisy." Some friends may call you "too fat" or "too thin." Your teachers may accuse you of being "too lazy" or "too inquisitive." Your parents may think you are "too active" or "too talkative." All these opinions form pictures in your mind about who you are. And these opinions usually carry a value of either "good" or "bad." When this information is fed or programmed into your memory, it significantly affects the way you look at yourself.

Ask yourself these questions:

1. Am I self-conscious? Why?

_____ .

2. How does self-consciousness affect me?

_____ .

3. Do I feel inner conflict because I am self-conscious?

_____ .

4. If so, what kind of conflict do I feel?

_____

_____ .

If self-consciousness does cause you conflict, you can be sure that there are many self-conscious people who also feel conflict.

Example:

Eric is self-conscious about being small. As a result, he works at appearing "tough." Debbie is self-conscious about being so tall and thin. As a result, she puts on a front of being superior and "hard-nosed." Whenever Eric and Debbie confront each other, they are not being themselves. They call each other names and never learn anything about one another.

Can you see how self-conscious people can come into conflict with each other because of the inner conflict they each feel?

Have you visited a foreign country? If you have, did you ever feel "out of place" or awkward? Why? Looking back at it now, can you identify ways you've been conditioned that affected how you saw yourself when in that foreign country? Can you identify ways you have been conditioned that affect how you view natives of the country you visited?

If you had a chance to go back to that country — or any country — name two steps you would take to change your thinking. How would you act differently?

1. _____ .

2. _____ .

Do you think these new actions would create less conflict for you?

Global Consciousness: How We See Others

Now let's move from looking at ourselves to examining the way we look at others, and how this can create conflict.

Prejudgment

Our brains can come to an incorrect conclusion because of limited information. For example, if the first tree you ever see in your life is a pine tree, then it is possible that, before you learn any differently, you think every tree in the world is called a pine tree. In your brain, the word "pine" means "tree." This is a harmless example of prejudging. Once you discover that there are other types of trees, your brain can make a simple adjustment.

If, however, your family is conditioned to believe that all Russians are warlike, and they have conditioned *you* to believe that all Russians are warlike — and you hold this to be true without examining it, then *you* are prejudging Russians. This kind of prejudgment can be very harmful. Can you see how?

Every time we see something new, and use previous information to label it, we are prejudging. This is the tendency of the brain: to compute new information based on the old. And our brain may not have a proper label for something that it is taking in for the first time. In this case, the brain may choose a label that comes closest to that which it knows.

What can we do about this? We can become AWARE of this process, and if our brain has chosen a label that we think might be incorrect, we can examine and correct it. At the very least, we can question it.

For example, have you ever met someone that you instantly disliked? Perhaps the person reminded you of someone that you had a conflict with in the past. Our memory can cause us to react this way. When this happens, it is important to catch your brain in the act and "correct" it. Your awareness leads you to think: "There's no reason to prejudge this new person."

Stereotyping

When the brain prejudges a person, it "stereotypes," which means it categorizes that person into a certain group — into a slot, a type, a pigeonhole. It is a dangerous way of thinking because it allows us to say things like, "Oh, he's just like any other teenager," without thoughtfully addressing the specific behavior of that particular person.

Examples of Stereotyped Thinking:

1. Eric committed a crime. Eric has red hair. Therefore, all persons with red hair are criminals.
2. John is stupid. John is black. Therefore, all black people are stupid.
3. Suzanne cries all the time. Why are women so emotional?
4. Arturo and Hans never show any emotion. Men are so unfeeling.

The conclusions reached above are examples of prejudiced, stereotypical beliefs. Can you see how prejudging in this way creates conflict in relationships? When we prejudge, we create a separation between ourselves and another person.

**If you catch yourself in the act of prejudging,
it's a sign that you are becoming AWARE.
You're beginning to see
how you have been conditioned.**

**This is a wonderful step,
because it means new learning is going on.
Once we look at our own prejudging and SEE it,
it can end.**

**Understanding how the brain prejudges
is an important step
in removing conflict from our lives.**

Repression

When we have painful thoughts and feelings, we often want to forget or bury them. So, we "repress" them. To repress means to hide from view, to pretend something doesn't exist. In the process, we create conflict, because repressed thoughts don't go away. They hide deep inside, stewing and bubbling beneath the surface.

When East Germans were finally allowed to travel to West Germany and other parts of the world in 1989, their repressed feelings and thoughts became known to the world via radio and television broadcasts. Their feelings had caused them great conflict and pain over many years. Gaining freedom of expression and movement has eased their conflict.

Example of Repressed Feelings:

Les never wanted to go boating and always became angry when Dale, his son, asked him to go. Dale didn't find out for many years that his father's brother drowned in a boating accident. It had been Les' idea to go boating on the day of the accident. Since his brother's death, Les had repressed his feelings and refused to discuss the accident.

Years later, Les agreed to go boating with Dale on the lake where Les' brother had died. Les cried afterward, finally allowing his repressed feelings to come to the surface.

Repressed thoughts and feelings accumulated from the past affect how we behave now. Even though Les was upset about something that happened a long time ago, it was affecting the way he treated Dale in the present.

Repressed feelings often come from self-judgment and the negative views we have about ourselves. This happens because people we trust have made us feel bad for feeling certain emotions, thinking certain thoughts, or acting in a particular way. So, we hide those feelings, thoughts and actions from our awareness. But hiding them doesn't solve the problem; it only makes it worse! There are some things you can do about this.

If you've never expressed painful feelings to someone you trust, this might be the time to do it. Repressed thoughts build up conflict inside of you, and this is one way to help yourself. Another is to understand how and why the brain represses, and how this causes conflict. Just being aware of this, especially as it happens, can help because awareness will prevent the brain from creating unnecessary conflict.

Projection and Scapegoating

Have you ever been blamed for something you didn't do? Have you ever blamed someone else for something you did? This is called projecting and making someone else a "scapegoat." This behavior can cause conflict in at least two ways: (1) it hurts another human being, and (2) it denies the truth.

Example of Projection:

Every four years, we witness the Republican and Democratic National Conventions on television. A candidate is selected to represent each party. After these conventions, we are inundated with TV ads for each candidate. As election time approaches, the ads become more and more insulting and accusing. Each party hurls blame and criticism onto the other.

The truth is that both parties are human beings capable of both top-notch and imperfect behavior. No amount of projection will change this.

If you have been guilty of projecting blame onto someone else, while knowing deep inside that you are also at fault, you are not dealing with the situation truthfully. You wind up hurting yourself as well as the other person. Projecting your own feelings onto someone else is learned behavior, and many of us are conditioned to do this. If you become AWARE of when you are projecting and stop yourself, this process will help change your conditioning.

Projection can also create "the enemy." When we repress negative, bad or hurtful thoughts and feelings about ourselves due to self-judgment, we often "project" those same thoughts and feelings onto other people, because then we can condemn what we have judged as "bad" and take it away from ourselves.

"*You* made me feel bad, and feeling bad is painful."
"*You* want to hurt me, therefore *you* are my enemy!" Projection can happen at the individual level, as well as at the group or national level. Understanding how we "create the enemy" through projection can have an effect on reducing conflict, inside yourself and globally.

Example of Scapegoating:

Devin spilled milk on the freshly washed kitchen floor. She was afraid she would be punished for it, so she blamed her baby brother, Dave, because she believed Dave would not be punished for the same act. By lying and placing blame on her innocent little brother, Devin did not take responsibility for an act she committed. Whether she meant to or not, she was the one who spilled the milk and the one who was responsible.

Spilling milk does not make Devin a bad person. It was an accident. Accepting responsibility might mean she would have to clean the floor or buy milk out of her allowance, but whatever the consequences, Devin would become a stronger person by owning up to what she did.

While spilling milk on the kitchen floor and blaming your younger brother does not create great harm, accusing another country of committing crimes they did not commit can be very destructive. It often, in fact, leads to war. And, while accusing a friend of being stupid or selfish when they have hurt your feelings may cause minor conflict between you, one country accusing another country of being stupid could lead to major conflict and war.

**When a group of people project
their conditioned fears and problems
onto another group of people,
conflict begins and war can follow.**

The Brain Maze

Any time we prejudge, repress, project or scapegoat, we create thoughts and feelings that are not true. One untruth is added to yet another, and in no time we get so far away from the heart of the matter that we can no longer find what the truth is. We wind up with a brain maze that ties our thoughts into a big knot.

Illustration of a "Brain Maze":

He is big.
He is to be feared.
I am afraid of him.
He must want to harm me.
He must be my enemy.
I will need to defend myself from him.
If he is the enemy, I must be the hero.
A hero is always right to defend against an enemy.
The enemy is bad.
The hero is good.
All heroes are right and good and must defend against enemies, who are wrong and bad.

Can you see how our brain's conditioning can cause conflict inside us? The more we allow this conflict to grow, the more likely we are to project our conflict onto other people. And if a lot of people in the world project their conflict onto others, do you see how we are likely to be faced with major global conflict — in other words, a war?

From Fear to War, in One Easy Lesson!

Fear
leads to
Negative Conditioned Thinking
leads to
Inner Conflict
leads to
Outer Conflict
leads to
Global Conflict

Chapter 9

DOES YOUR BRAIN KNOW
WHO YOU ARE?

You now know that conditioning affects the way you think and act. Are you aware that it also affects the way you look? If you were to ask yourself the question, "Who am I?" what would your answer be? There isn't any right or wrong answer. We all have self-images based on who we think we are. I'm sure there are kids at your school who have a very obvious self-image.

Do you have a self-image? What is it? How do you see yourself? It's important to ask yourself these questions, because a self-image not only determines how you see yourself, it also determines how you see others.

What is a Self-Image?

A self-image is a picture you have about yourself. Sometimes your self-image is positive and sometimes it's negative. The way you see yourself can vary from day to day — sometimes hour to hour. If you're like me, there are times when you look at yourself and don't like what you see at all! Conditioning plays a big part in how you see yourself.

I'm sure there are times when you wish you were someone else — perhaps a rock star, a movie star, a great athlete, a humanitarian, or some person you admire. You may dress to present a certain self-image. There are lots of different "looks."

Do you know people who fit these images?

The Californian (Surfer)
The Preppy (Class President)
The Rock Star (Punk Rocker)
The Most Popular (Cheerleader)
The Super Jock (Football Player)
The Academic Achiever (Nerd)

Can you think of other "looks"? People dress to match these images because they feel it makes a statement about who they are, or gives them a sense of belonging to a group or "clique." Young adults like you often experiment with these looks, changing from one to another in an exploration of themselves.

Sometimes this exploration continues when students graduate and head for the job market. They dress in a certain way to get a position they want, or to become part of a certain group. As they get older, they sometimes change their "type" because it no longer represents who they feel they are or want to be. There are many corporate executive "preppies" who used to dress like "hippies."

A Conditioned Self-Image Can Cause Conflict

The problem with self-images is that they can lead to conflict — not always, but particularly when people believe that their image is superior to others. Or when people believe that their way is the only way. If you are a punk rocker and you've decided you don't like preppies, you are creating conflict

85

between you and other people — even if it's only in your mind. It's the "good guy/bad guy" routine. This kind of thinking divides human beings.

Example:

Imagine that the color RED looks at the color BLUE and decides not to like it because it isn't RED. (Does that sound as thoughtless to you as it does to me?)

Now, imagine Lucy, the PUNK ROCKER, looks at Manny, the PREPPY, and decides not to like him because he isn't a PUNK ROCKER. (That's just as thoughtless, isn't it?)

You may say, "So what if Lucy doesn't like Manny? It's hard to like everybody!" What's important to see is that Lucy is reacting to Manny out of negative conditioning, and is not responding to who Manny really is. This kind of conditioned thinking can lead to the following:

Imagine that THE UNITED STATES OF AMERICA declares war on RUSSIA because of that country's differing lifestyle.

Can you see the danger in believing that there are "right" and "wrong" images? Let's explore what happens in your brain when you think this way.

Think of a time when you reacted negatively to someone because of what they were wearing, how they spoke, or how they looked. On the next page, describe the situation...

A. The situation was:

_____ .

B. Name three reasons why you reacted the way you did:

   1. _____ .

   2. _____ .

   3. _____ .

C. Were any of these reasons based on a fear you had?

_____ .

D. What was your fear? If you can't think of any examples, see if any of these fit your situation:

   1. I was afraid my friend looked better than I did.
   2. I was afraid that my clothes weren't good enough.
   3. I was afraid because she was new in town and she was different.
   4. I was afraid my friends would make fun of me.
   5. I was afraid I'd lose my friends if I didn't make fun with them.

I was afraid because:

_____ .

Why do *you* think kids sometimes make fun of how other kids dress, talk, think, or act? What do you think causes a kid to think his or her way of dressing or acting is better than someone else's way?

Our Thinking is Affected by Our "Conditioning"

If you guessed that this kind of behavior comes from your "conditioning," you guessed right. Who was the last person who gave you a hard time about the way you dressed or talked? How did you react? Did you get angry? Walk away? Ignore the remark?

Understand that this person is not "bad." He or she has been "conditioned" to believe that there is a right and wrong way to be, and does not understand that this kind of thinking creates conflict.

The thoughts, "I am better than…," or "She is better than…," or "You are wrong, and I am right!" may exist only in our minds, but these thoughts easily translate into actions. If you are thinking, "He is wrong and I am right," you are creating a "villain" and you are going to project this *attitude* whenever you talk to that person. There will be conflict between you, and you may not even be aware that it is coming from you.

Conflict may also be created in the process of *identifying* with a hero you admire. For example, let's say you imagine yourself as the main character in a film you see. The reality of this situation, however, is that the character is only an image on the screen, and does not really exist. It is like grasping for air!

90

Perhaps you see someone in school and *identify* with her. You think, "If I could just be like her, I'd be happy." But how well do you know her? Maybe she has more problems than you do. Maybe she would secretly like to be like you!

**We do harm to ourselves in attempting to
live up to an image —
not only because it's living a lie,
but because it limits us and keeps us from
being who we are.**

Trying to be like someone else causes conflict inside us: "I'm not her, but I want to be like her." It's painful and gets you nowhere.

Conflict is caused by:

1. Creating a "villain": looking down on, making fun of, or feeling superior to someone; making someone wrong, and insisting on being right — or

2. Creating a "hero": identifying with a movie star or someone you admire, trying to live up to an image of someone who does not really exist.

We are conditioned by our friends, family, religion, government, culture, and the media. Our conditioning is expressed through our clothes, language, the food we eat, our education. Have you ever looked at the total "image" of yourself? Let's begin!

On a piece of paper, write your name. After reading each heading (1 - 10) following, fill in a short answer that describes yourself. Yuki's answers are given as an example.

Name: (Yuki Hamada)
1. Favorite Clothes:
   (*Blue jeans, sweaters, black and white silk*)
2. Language:
   (*English and Japanese*)
3. Favorite Foods:
   (*Veggie-burgers, taco chips and vanilla milkshakes*)
4. Best Friends:
   (*Bobby, Phyllis, Robin and Peg*)
5. Family:
   (*Mother, father, two brothers, several aunts, uncles, cousins, grandparents*)
6. Education:
   (*Grammar school, junior high and high school; piano lessons, Spanish lessons*)
7. Religion:
   (*I don't believe in Heaven or Hell.*)
8. Culture:
   (*My Japanese heritage has provided my family with many customs and traditions.*)
9. Government:
   (*I'm not sure I agree with the government. Sometimes it feels as if politicians don't tell us the truth. I'd like to be a Senator one day.*)

10. Media:
    (*I watch public-sponsored television and news broadcasts.
    I listen to rock on the radio.*)

Compare your answers with Yuki's? Is she different from you? How so? Do you think the fact that you are different would keep you from being friends? Would it interest you to get to know Yuki? Why? Do you think people want to be "different"?

1. How does a positive self-image affect you?

_____ .

2. How does a negative self-image affect you?

_____ .

3. How does a self-image limit you?

_____ .

The reason I ask you these questions is that I feel it's important for you to get to know yourself! We often don't take the time to really know who we are. When you become familiar with your own image, you can more easily understand where many of your beliefs and attitudes come from.

Have you heard the phrase, "You are what you eat"? I think there's some truth to that. I also believe that:

"You are what you think."

Chapter 10

YOU ARE WHAT YOU THINK

Different "Looks"
Can Lead To Different Beliefs

As we get older, our "looks" or "self-images" tend to expand into more than just a different way of dressing or combing our hair. Our "identities" develop into values and beliefs which, over a period of time, become ingrained habits and traditions. Our looks reflect our beliefs. Here is an example:

Doug wears "preppy" clothes; his hair is always neatly combed. He doesn't drink, smoke or take drugs. He is a top athlete. Doug thinks, "I am proud that I go to the best prep school around. I do what is right and acceptable. I study hard and expect to go to a top university so I can become a highly paid professional. I believe that my country's political view of economic expansion is the best in the world. I go to church and believe that my God is the only God, and that my religion is the only true religion."

When Doug grows up, he works for a well-known law firm, does what he is expected to do, and gets regular promotions. He and his wife belong to the local country club, drive a Volvo station wagon and spend their summers on Cape Cod. They have two children: a boy named Lance and a girl named Muffy. Doug plans to send his children to the very best prep schools and colleges so that they will do well in life.

Dorathy, who went to the same prep school as Doug, has a different "view." She wears military looking clothes; her hair is cut short and is shaved at the sides. She is involved in the peace movement and marches against her country's involvement in fighting overseas. Dorathy thinks, "The prep school my parents forced me to go to was too conservative. I believe in challenging authority and questioning my country's political and economic policies. I want to work for human and animal rights and don't believe in making money for my personal pleasure. Making money just creates competition and conflict. I don't go to church but believe in a higher being which I come into contact with through meditation."

Dorathy works for a women's liberation organization and is active in the equal rights and pro-choice movements. She lives in a converted warehouse with a group of activists in San Francisco. She is not married and has no children, choosing instead to devote her life to poor kids who live in her city.

Doug and Dorathy meet at their high school reunion ten years after graduation. They get into a heated argument over men's and women's roles. Doug believes that women should be full-time homemakers and devote themselves to the family and the raising of children — that this is an extremely valuable contribution to society. Dorathy

95

believes that this view has led to the oppression of women, and that it is essential to break through this confining stereotype so that women can reach their creative and professional potential.

Doug and Dorathy have different beliefs. Each one thinks the other is "wrong" and each one holds on to his or her own belief as the "right" one. Most people have good reasons for their beliefs. Any time you look at a person and see a difference, or something that sets you apart from that person, you can make a decision, right then and there, not to jump to any conclusions. You can decide to learn something instead.

Your conditioned thinking is creating the conflict.

The way to a peaceful world is to sit down with one another, discuss our conflicts, and reach an understanding about the basic causes of our conflicts — so that our disagreements do not lead to more fighting. This may not be the easiest path, but I believe it is the most helpful one in the long run.

The keys to solving conflict are:
1. Becoming more *aware* of who we are;
2. *Understanding* how our brains have been conditioned to act in certain ways;
3. *Exploring* the causes of our conflicts.

Understanding each other must be the number one priority at school and at home. The next time you look at someone you think is "different," consider:

1. What am I doing to this relationship when I focus on our differences?
2. What would happen if I focused on our similarities?

Beliefs and Attitudes

Let's take a look at some beliefs and attitudes commonly held by people in the world today. You already know that a belief is an opinion — sometimes true and sometimes not — that we are conditioned to accept. Here are some examples:

1. I *believe* that people should respect and defend their country, no matter what.
2. I *believe* that going to church makes me a good person.
3. My *attitude* toward war is that it is necessary in order to keep the peace.
4. My *attitude* is that life should be peaceful and loving.

Attitudes and beliefs are handed down from generation to generation. You've learned most of the ones you have from your parents, grandparents, and other people who helped bring you up. Those that were taught to you when you were very young, you've come to accept without question. When we are young, we are very impressionable and easily conditioned. We grow up with those attitudes and beliefs that we encounter on a daily basis. Day by day, the beliefs we are taught sink in and become part of us — part of our conditioning.

The beliefs you have can change, provided you are aware, have reached an understanding, and are open to new information. It's beneficial to listen to other people express their points of view, because they may have reasons for their beliefs that could be important to you.

Example:

Ted's parents believe that fighting back is the only way to handle a bully. Ted believed this too.

Gary's parents believe that you should "turn the other cheek" if a bully strikes you, and that the only way to achieve peace is by making peace. Gary believes this too.

Ted had dinner at Gary's house one night and heard Gary's family's point of view. It made sense to him, and he now agrees with Gary.

As we have seen, traditions, attitudes and beliefs make up what we think, and consist of information we have gathered from family, friends, school, the community, and the media (TV, movies, radio, books, newspapers and magazines). It is important for us to make friends, look at how they live, and listen to what they believe. Sometimes we discover that how and what we think may not be the best for us or for others. As you already know, what we think and how we act can create conflict.

Some beliefs and attitudes have been around for a long time, but this doesn't mean they're true. Which of the following beliefs do you think are true? As you read each one, think about how you feel about it. You may want to discuss these with your parents, your friends, or in your classroom.

1. "Might is right." If you are powerful, then you are right. The more weapons a country has, the stronger and better it is.

2. "An eye for an eye." If someone hits you, you ought to hit back. If someone calls you a name, you should call a name back. If a person is mean to you, you should be just as mean.

3. "My country, right or wrong." Many people feel it is their patriotic responsibility to defend their country, even if they personally believe that their country is guilty of faulty judgment or behavior.

These beliefs have been around for centuries, and a lot of people hold them to be true. Do you agree with these beliefs? I feel that they provoke conflict and violence. Can you see how?

When we act out of fear, and react negatively to someone who is different from us, we are experiencing conflict and the foundations of war. When fear is present, conflict is not far behind. And when conflict is present, war is sure to rear its ugly head.

Fear,
A Conditioned Response
leads to
Conflict,
A Conditioned Response
leads to
War,
A Conditioned Response

It may be new for you to explore your beliefs and attitudes. It may be new for you to consider if what you have been taught at home or in school is true — or not. What matters most is that you question, and that you realize the importance of questioning.

Perhaps you've been discouraged from asking questions. Perhaps there have been times when you asked questions and didn't get answers. If so, remember that you can always ask questions and think them through for yourself. Many of the questions we ask don't have fixed answers — and sometimes just by exploring the question, we reach an understanding. I feel that arriving at an understanding can be far more valuable than accepting a fixed answer.

Chapter 11

COMPARING WAYS OF THINKING

In school we are taught what to think, but schools rarely teach us what thinking is. Have you ever stopped to really look at your thinking?

When you are working on a science project or constructing a model, you start with something basic and build on it. When you are building a house, you lay a foundation, then a layer of bricks, one level at a time, until — bingo! — you have a building!

This kind of systematic thinking and action is applied every day in solving mechanical, scientific and technological problems. For instance, when you move from a big house into a smaller one, you have to figure out how to make the old furniture fit into the smaller house. This takes thinking and figuring.

However, the kind of thinking we've been looking at here is psychological. When we become aware of how two differently conditioned people respond to the same situation, we develop an understanding of the fact that there is more than one way to look at almost anything. The following example illustrates this point.

The Situation:

1. Howard and Patrick find out that there was a party last night, and...

2. Many of their friends were there.
3. The party was at Debbie's house.
4. Patrick and Howard were not invited to the party.

Howard Thinks:

1. There was a party at Debbie's house. I was not invited.
2. If I was not invited, it must mean that Debbie doesn't want to socialize with me.
3. If Debbie doesn't want to socialize with me, it must mean that she doesn't like me.
4. If she doesn't like me, there must be something wrong with me.
5. If there is something wrong with me, I guess I deserve to be alone.
6. If I try to make friends, I'll just be rejected.

Patrick Thinks:

1. There was a party at Debbie's house. I was not invited.
2. If I was not invited, there must be a good reason.
3. I don't think Debbie has my phone number.
4. I'll have to give Debbie my telephone number.
5. I like Debbie and I don't want to miss her parties.
6. Maybe I'll have a party next week and invite her.

Whatever the reason that Debbie didn't call Howard and Patrick, each has his own interpretation of the same situation. Each one's thinking brought him to the conclusion he reached, before either found out what the real reason was. Let's take a look at Howard and Patrick's thinking...

1. How does Howard's thinking differ from Patrick's?

_____ .

2. Do you have some clues as to Howard's conditioning and self-image?

_____ .

3. Do you have some clues as to Patrick's conditioning and self-image?

_____ .

4. Do you see how two people can draw entirely different conclusions from the same incident?

_____ .

5. Did you relate to Howard, or did you relate to Patrick?

_____ .

6. Why do you think you related to the one you chose?

_____ .

Let's look at another set of circumstances. Consider the following larger, more dangerous situation...

The Situation:

Country #1 and Country #2 discover that Country #3 has nuclear missile bases located very close to them.

Country #1 Thinks:

1. Country #3 has secretly placed nuclear missiles near us.
2. Country #3 has a lot of nerve.
3. Country #3 must be planning to attack us.
4. Country #3 probably wants to take over.
5. Country #3 has another thing coming.
6. We will place our missiles so they are in strategic positions, ready for the next move.

Country #2 Thinks:

1. Country #3 has secretly placed nuclear missiles near us.
2. Country #3 must be frightened of us.
3. Country #3 must think we're going to attack it.
4. I wonder where Country #3 got that idea.
5. We better get in contact with Country #3 and arrange a meeting to find out what this is all about.
6. Let's make disarmament the priority topic of conversation.

Let's look at the thinking of Country #1 and #2:

1. How does Country #1's thinking differ from that of Country #2's?

2. Do you have clues as to #1's national conditioning?

_____ .

3. Do you have clues as to #2's national conditioning?

_____ .

4. Do you see how representatives of different countries can draw different conclusions from the same incident?

_____ .

5. Did you relate to Country #1 or Country #2? Why?

_____

_____ .

When we see a situation from only one side, we increase the chances for conflict.

Conditioned to be "Good"

I want to tell you about the effects of conditioning on a boy named John Parsons. John was taught to be "a good boy." There was no room for John to have any "bad" behavior, and this may be the cause of what happened.

John was an Eagle Scout at the age of 13, and an altar boy at his church. He was a straight "A" student, captain of the

Junior Varsity team, and President of his class. He was kind to older people and pleasant to be around. Everyone liked him.

That's why it was difficult for people who knew him to accept the headlines in the local newspaper. Everyone was shocked. The headline read: "Local Student, John Parsons, Arrested for Drug Theft and Assault Charges."

The newspaper reported:

"At 12:02 Friday afternoon, 14-year-old John Parsons of Oak City was arrested for driving a stolen vehicle, driving under the influence of drugs, and assaulting the arresting officer of the law. Found in the car were traces of drug equipment, a loaded "38" police special revolver and a box of pornographic magazines. Apparently he was selling drugs and sex magazines to local junior high school students...."

"I can't believe John Parsons could do anything like that," said his principal, Doris Davis, of Bingham Junior High. "John is the best student we have. He always has the highest grades. It makes no sense what he did."

"This is impossible. Not John! John is very religious. He has very high moral standards. He even told me that he wanted to become a minister of God so he could fight the devil," said Reverend Ken Brown, John's minister.

Studies of young people like John reveal that underneath their "perfect" behavior they are angry, disturbed and violent because they have been hiding their true feelings, afraid that their families and friends would not accept them. Sometimes their "release" from these "wrong" or "bad" feelings is to commit violent acts.

Many girls and boys are highly conditioned to do the "right" thing, to live "properly," to always "be good," to get "perfect" grades in school. Do you know anyone like this?

There are some truths that are true for everyone. Well, here is one of them:

"Nobody is perfect."

The desire to be perfect creates great conflict within us. We are torn between who we think we should be and the reality of who we are. If you've been expecting perfection from yourself, you probably have a lot of conflict built up inside you. It is important to know that nobody is perfect. Let's explore some ways *you* have been taught to be "good."

Exercise 1:

Name three ways you've been conditioned to be "good":

A. _____ .

B. _____ .

C. _____ .

1. Can you think of ways the above conditioning has caused you conflict?   If so, how?

   _____

   _____ .

2. Do you see any way of resolving this conflict?

   Name three people with whom you would consider discussing your conflict:

   A. _____ .

   B. _____ .

   C. _____ .

   How do you think each one of these people would react?

   A. _____ .

   B. _____ .

   C. _____ .

Exercise 2:

Create a "roleplay" situation with one of these people. You can roleplay yourself and ask friends (also roleplayed by you) for their opinions. You might begin like this:

You: "I want to ask your opinion. I'm very upset because I want to do what my parents tell me to do, but I want to get revenge on this guy who wrecked my bike, and my parents say I should just forget about it — that it's not worth it. What do you think I should do?"

Friend #1: "I think you should beat him up, teach him a lesson."

Friend #2: "I think you should just forget about it, like your parents say."

Friend #3: "How did he wreck your bike? Did he mean to do it?"

Friend #4: "What would make you feel better about the situation?"

Friend #5: "Can you reason with this guy? Can you ask him to get the bike fixed?"

Friends can often give you ideas about how to deal with problems.

Another way to "roleplay" is to ask one of your friends to roleplay as you, and you roleplay as one of the people you would like to talk to. You say the things you think they would say to you, and your friend responds as you might.

Exercise 3:

Compare your thinking with the way your friends think. Get together with one or more friends, and each of you write on a piece of paper:

"I believe being 'good' means..."

After you are done writing, read what you have written out loud to each other. Look at the ways you all agree, and the ways you don't agree. See if you can come up with a "group" definition of what it means to be "good" — a definition that pleases everyone.

Star Wars:
An Outcome of Conditioned Thinking

To the United States and many other countries, being "good" means being strong — the best, the world leader, the top banana. To military organizations, being the best means having the latest and largest collection of weapons.

Our latest war machine (in the planning stage) is right out of science fiction. It's called "Star Wars" (or SDI). This shield would be placed in space and would involve thousands of orbiting battle stations that could destroy at least 10,000 "enemy" weapons travelling at about 20,000 miles per hour. Star Wars, created to stop nuclear weapons from hitting their targets, would be supposedly 90-95% effective, which means that only 5-10% of nuclear weapons could get through. But "only 5%" could kill as many as 100 million people!

Star Wars involves the largest military expenditure of money ever. It could cost one-trillion dollars! Do you know how much one-trillion dollars is? It is one-million dollars a day for the next 2,730 years! If you could count a trillion $1 bills, one per second, 24 hours per day, it would take 32,000 years!

To put it differently, one-trillion dollars could buy a $100,000 furnished house for every family in Kansas, Missouri, Nebraska, Oklahoma and Iowa. Then you could put a $10,000 car in the garage of each house. There would still be money left over to build 10 one-million dollar libraries and 10 one-million dollar hospitals for 250 cities in those states, and there would still be enough money left over to build 10 one-million dollar schools for 500 communities. Would you believe that there would still be enough money left in the bank to pay 10,000 nurses and teachers just from the interest alone, plus give a

$5,000 bonus to every family in those states each year —
forever?

War is incredibly expensive. Did you know that one
modern fighter plane can cost $50,000,000 — that's fifty-million
dollars?! Did you know that 5% of the military budget could
take every child out of poverty?

Who pays for this? Your parents, your teachers and your
adult friends. And when you are old enough to earn a living,
you will be paying for it. All earning adults are required to pay
taxes to the government from the money they make in their
day-to-day work, and the government spends a large proportion
of this money on weapons and the military. So, we are all
directly or indirectly involved in the proliferation of weapons in
preparation for war. All because we cannot resolve our
conflicts!

The Beating You Know You Will Get
A Story

You are on the school playground. It's almost dusk and no
one else is there. All the teachers have left. Even the school
custodian has locked up and gone home for the day. You've
been waiting, hoping that Eric has forgotten, but you feel he is
lurking somewhere. You've been stopped by him before and
you've managed to run away, but this time you can't. During
basketball practice, you hurt your ankle.

Everything seems peaceful, so you decide to go. You begin
to walk across the playground from your lookout place behind
the equipment shed. The school outdoor light has just come
on. Home is eight long blocks away. Between school and home
are open fields, scattered houses and a few trees.

You recall the incident that happened earlier that day when you were in the boys' bathroom, and Eric and two of his buddies walked in. You were combing your hair when you saw their reflection in the mirror.

"There he is, Mr. Pretty Boy. Can't get away from me now. I told ya' I'd catch up with you, punk. And so here we are, just you and me."

"And your buddies!" you shout back out of fear and anger.

"Don't mouth off, jerk, or I'll pulverize you. Now give me your wallet. I know you're loaded. Hand it over or I'll turn you over to these guys. They can do the dirty work since you ain't worth my effort anyhow!"

"Look, Eric..." you begin to say, feeling your knees getting weak and your mouth dry. You feel a little like throwing up.

"Ring!" The bell goes off, signaling the start of a new class period. In bursts three senior football players. You dart out the door and run down the corridor to your classroom.

"I'll get ya' later!" Eric shouts after you.

You are not a fighter. Your parents have told you to solve your problems peacefully, but they haven't shown you how. You feel the conflict burning inside you. You want to be "good" but you also want to take care of yourself.

You continue now across the empty playground and into the school corridor. Your footsteps echo loudly off the concrete walls. You feel tension in your whole being. Your fists are clenched, and you are listening intently for any sound. Suddenly you hear a noise behind you, like a locker closing. You freeze. Your palms feel sweaty and cold. Your fingers ache from making fists. You hear slow, quiet footsteps moving toward you. Your legs feel like lead, as if they are magnetized

to the floor. With all your effort, you try to run, but it feels like you're in deep sand. Your ankle hurts, and you are half-running, half-limping.

You make it across the empty parking lot, not wanting to look behind you for fear of what may be there. The footsteps are getting closer, and there is more than one pair of them. As you reach the open field, you trip on the rough dirt and fall into the wet, green grass. You get up quickly, your nose a little bloody from bumping it when you fell. You want to scream for help, but there is no one to hear you. You start to cry as you hobble across the field, wishing you could stand and face Eric and his bully friends.

Suddenly your feet go out from under you and you go down again. Someone has tackled you from behind and holds your face down on the ground with your arm pinned painfully behind your back. Your face is covered with sweat, blood and dirt. You are pulled to your feet and stand weakly in front of Eric and his two buddies.

Eric is angry, his face as red as his hair. He pulls you up by your collar so that you have to stand on tiptoes to him. You feel sick and start to cry. You await the beating you know you are going to get.

Chapter 12

ALTERNATIVES TO FIGHTING

What could you do to change the situation described in "The Beating You Know You Will Get"? You are conditioned to run away, but your ankle hurts. Anyway, you've run away before and that didn't feel good either. It makes you feel weak, and the other kids call you "chicken." Your parents have told you to "turn the other cheek." If you do this, you'll still get punched — on both cheeks! Even if you tried to fight, you'd get beaten up because you don't know how to defend yourself. Any way you look at it, you lose. Talk about conflict! This is it.

The way it looks right now, you have two alternatives: You can fight. Or you can run. But this fight or flight response is like a double-edged sword — both sides can hurt you.

Have you ever been in this situation? Have you been bullied? Have you been afraid of getting beaten up? Have you ever felt that you could not handle a bully and then been ashamed because you couldn't? If your answer to all these questions is "yes," you are not alone. There are thousands of kids and adults who have been in this same situation.

The Day of the Bee Sting

I got into that situation often while I was growing up. I lived in a rough neighborhood and was bullied a lot, and used to run home frightened. I am 50 years old, yet the memory of

2. **Psychological confidence.** Nonviolent alternatives allow you to act intelligently and peacefully in potentially harmful situations, because the fight/flight response is prevented from coming into play. When you are not "re-acting" from this fight/flight response, then there is a "space," a moment where there is no fear. This fearless space allows for an intelligent response to a threat. So it is important to learn nonviolent alternatives to conflict. The latter part of this chapter explains some nonviolent alternatives that will help you to protect yourself.

Nonviolent Alternatives

If you are planning to study Karate, or some other art of self-defense, it is important that you also learn the art of nonviolent alternatives, because they are two parts of a whole. The ability to defend yourself physically is only half the art; the ability to use nonviolent alternatives is the other half. Combined, they allow you to face any threat. When a threat comes, and the "old brain" triggers the response "Fight!" or "Run!" — your new brain will ask, "Can I handle this threat?" And the answer will be, "Yes."

This "yes" creates a pause, a space in which you don't have to fight or run away. It is a short meditation space from which you can STOP, LOOK, LISTEN and decide which nonviolent alternative to use to resolve the threatening situation.

These alternatives are dealt with more fully in this book's companion book, entitled *Facing The Double-Edged Sword*, but here are a few, briefly described, that you can try when faced with a bully:

1. **Make friends.** Treat the bully as a friend; he probably doesn't have very many. ("Hi, Eric. Where did you get that great bike? What model is it?")

2. **Use humor.** Don't make fun of the bully, but make fun of the situation. ("I'd really enjoy a nice fight now, Eric, but frankly I'm late for dinner. Bye.") ("This is a joke, me fighting you. You're too good for me. There's no way I could win. Want to go bowling instead?")

3. **Trick him.** Pretend you are sick or that you are about to meet someone. ("My brother's a policeman, and he's meeting me around the corner in two minutes. Bye.")

4. **Walk away.** Refuse to comply with his wishes. Turn around and walk away confidently.

5. **Agree.** If the bully says you are a wimp, agree with him. Don't let it get you angry. ("You're right, Eric. I'm the weakest person in the world. I'm a wimp. You're right, okay? Everybody knows it. So what's the good of fighting? What are you going to prove? I've gotta go.")

6. **Refuse to fight.** No matter what, don't fight! ("You can hit me if you want to, but I'm not going to fight you, Eric. I don't believe in fighting. Is there a problem? Let's talk.")

7. **Scream or yell.** A loud yell can distract the bully so you can get away.

8. **Take a Karate stance.** If you know Karate, take a combat stance. Hopefully you won't have to use this alternative, but if you do, it will let the bully know you are prepared to defend yourself. But use this alternative only as a last resort. If you really think carefully about how to get out of conflict nonviolently, you most likely will never have to take a stance!

There are other alternatives, but these give you an idea of the possibilities. Understanding the alternatives adds to your repertoire and confidence. When you have confidence, fear caused by a threat to your physical well-being is lessened so the threat can be handled more successfully. Confidence gives you a chance to find creative, less violent solutions.

Using Nonviolent Alternatives in Response to Psychological Threats

It is difficult for the brain to tell the difference between fantasy (e.g. images of war on TV) and reality (e.g. real war). So, you may feel threatened by the images of violence you see on TV, and your body may respond with the "fight or flight" reaction. Your "old brain" produces fear and your body responds as if the threat were real. Your heart pumps fast, and energy is produced to help you fight or run away.

While the threat is only *psychological*, it is perceived as an actual physical need to protect yourself, to be a warrior. TV

122

and movie images create and reinforce the feeling that you are surrounded by "enemies." Your brain wants to resolve these threats, but it can't.

Contemplation as a Way to Observe Thinking

There is a type of thinking that you are using right now, called "intellectual thinking." As you read the words, there is a quiet observation process going on in which you are allowing words on a page to enter your brain and become images.

The process of contemplation is similar. Perhaps you have seen someone meditate; it looks like they are resting while sitting up. Meditation or contemplation involves sitting quietly, observing thinking, and can help you slow down your thoughts so you can see how they affect your actions. Meditation acts like a mirror; it can help you look at, be aware of, and observe yourself. This is how you do it:

1. Find a quiet place to sit, away from distractions.

2. Sit in a chair or on the floor, either cross-legged or with legs in a comfortable position. Keep your back straight and breathe normally.

3. Just watch your thoughts. One of the best ways to quiet your mind and slow down your thinking is to pay attention to your breathing. As you sit in a quiet place, notice the way your breath comes in and out of your body.

4. As you become aware of this, start counting your breaths — 1, 2, 3 — all the way to 10, then start again. If you find you have passed 10, merely be aware of it and start over at 1.

5. Try this for one or two minutes. Every day, increase the time a little. This exercise helps you become calm and allows you to look at your thinking.

6. Then meditate without counting your breaths. Just watch your thoughts arise in your brain like bubbles in a glass of soda. Don't dwell on them. Just let them come and go.

When you meditate, many thoughts will come into your mind. They may seem to be bits and pieces of floating information that have no connection or meaning by themselves. These thoughts are like daydreams. Everyday thoughts may enter your mind, such as, "I wonder what's for lunch?" or "I forgot to do my homework!" You may also have thoughts that fill you with emotion, such as "Why did Mom yell at me?" or "I hate it when my brother does that."

Powerful emotional thoughts can be de-charged by this process. Repressed anger ("Why didn't Dad let me go to the party?") or repressed self-conscious thoughts ("Why am I so ugly?" or "I wish I were taller, smarter, a better student, an athlete!") may come up in your meditation. If they do, just let them; don't judge your thoughts or feelings as "good" or "bad." *Just watch*, and see if you can learn something about how they may be causing conflict inside you.

Awakening From a Nightmare

If you see a violent movie or read a frightening book and then go to sleep, you may have bad dreams. There is something you can do.

1. When you wake up from a nightmare, sit quietly and calm your mind by counting your breaths. Focus your attention on your breathing and count from 1 to 10 and over again. Do this for a few minutes until the frightening images begin to fade.

2. After you feel calm, recall the dream. Watch the images in your brain as if you were watching a movie or program on television. Look at them as if they are nothing more than images on a screen — and remind yourself that they cannot hurt you.

3. Realize that you have control over these images.

   A. See the frightening image come up. If it's a person, talk to that person.
   B. Tell "it" that you are not afraid.
   C. Tell "it" a joke to make it laugh.
   D. See if you can change the image in your mind. If it's big, make it small. If if has a mean or violent look, make it gentle and loving.

In the same way that you develop confidence to deal with a bully in a physically threatening situation, you can develop confidence to deal with your fears, nightmares, or other frightening circumstances. Perhaps it will surprise you to discover that you have control over frightening images. And the truth is, you really do. The more you experience this, the more confident you'll become, and the easier it will be to deal with your fears the next time.

**If we all feel fear, and act out of fear,
it's no wonder there is so much conflict in the world!**

Exercise:

Name three situations that frighten you:

1. _____ .

2. _____ .

3. _____ .

Pick one of the above situations to meditate on. Go through the meditation process, then write your thoughts down on a piece of paper. Did the meditation help? What thoughts came to your mind? Were you able to think your fears through and come up with possible ways to resolve them?

Re-Creating Thoughts

When you meditate, sit quietly and simply allow your mind to do its thing. You don't have to take any action. All you have to do is watch, as if you are watching a program on television.

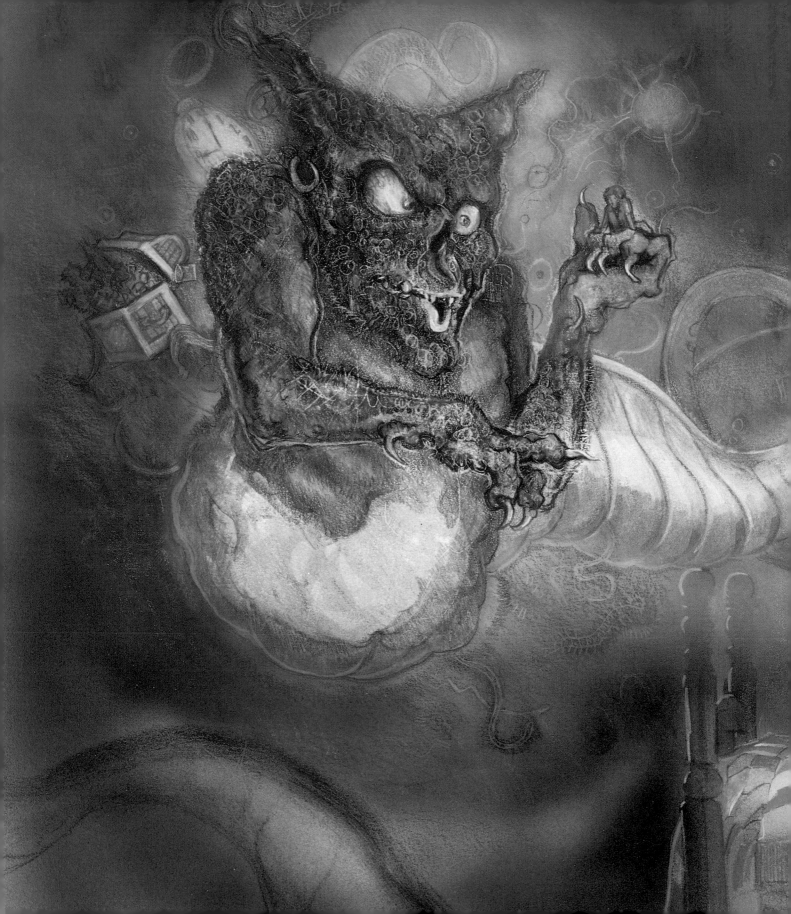

It is important for you to understand that:

1. You are the creator of these thoughts at this moment.
2. You are responsible for these thoughts.

Once you accept responsibility for your thoughts, you have three choices:

A. You can ACT on these thoughts.

   - OR -

B. You can NOT ACT on these thoughts.

   - OR -

C. You can change these thoughts.

Meditation allows you to think about a problem or situation and work it through in your mind — before you act. As a result, this creative thinking sometimes resolves the conflict in your mind, so that you don't have to take an action that will produce conflict. Meditation can put an end to painful thoughts before they go any further.

Exercise #1:

Before your meditation, you are upset:
Your mom yelled at you and you are angry.

As you begin your meditation, first concentrate on your breathing to calm yourself down. Then, after you feel calm, begin to look at the problem. Ask yourself why your mom yelled at you. Go over all the ways you may have upset her. Then go over all the other things that happened in the day that might have upset her.

You see that your mom is under a lot of pressure right now. You think about your anger and how it hurt your feelings when she yelled at you. You decide to tell her your feelings were hurt and to apologize for upsetting her, and to ask if she needs any help.

When you come out of your meditation, you feel much calmer, and you have worked out an approach to the conflict you were feeling before you meditated.

Exercise #2:

Remember when we were imagining the conflict you might feel if your father wouldn't let you go to a party? Do you think you can think of a way to resolve that situation now? How would you go about it?

Remember when we were discussing the conflict you might feel if someone came to the door asking to use your phone because their car had stalled, and your parents had instructed you never to open the door to a stranger? Can you think of a resolution now?

Exercise #3:

Earlier, we talked about the conditioned thought:
All Russians are warlike. We created a situation in which

your parents, conditioned to believe that all Russians are warlike, conditioned you to believe the same thing. (This was used as an example of prejudging.)

What kind of thought and action do you think it would take to move you from the thought:

1. All Russians are warlike.

   - TO -

2. Some Russians are warlike.

   - TO -

3. I wonder how many Russians are warlike.

   - TO -

4. What makes a person "warlike"?

Getting Conditioned to the Truth

Superman is portrayed as a hero who fights for "truth, justice and the American way." There are a lot of differently conditioned people in this world, and each person has his or her idea of what "truth" means. One person's hero might not be another person's hero. The "truth" to one person may not be the "truth" to another. The Catholics have their truth, and the Jews have theirs. The Arabs have their truth, and the Israelis have theirs. Your parents have theirs and you have yours.

"Justice" means one thing to a murderer and something entirely different to the family of a murder victim. The

American way is just that — the American way. The Russians, Chinese, Africans, Australians, Japanese all have their way, which, to them, is the "right" way.

The older we get, the more seriously we take our thoughts, it seems. And the more serious the conflict inside us, the more serious the actions we take, and the more serious the consequences. The Arabs and the Israelis are a dramatic example. The walls that exist between people — between Russians and Americans, between Palestinians and Jews, Buddhists and Moslems — are constructed of words, ideas and concepts. The conflicts between these people are created by how and what they think.

Understanding your thinking and the conflict it creates helps you understand all thinking and the conflict that can arise from it.

Do you agree with this statement?

**"If you figure out how your conditioned thinking
creates barriers between you and people you know,
then you have taken an important step toward
understanding the global barriers
that nations and religions create.**

**Nations and religions are just communities of people.
Therefore, if you can understand individual conflict,
you can understand world conflict."**

Chapter 13

GOING BEYOND YOUR CONDITIONING

Television Advertising

You are familiar with a few nonviolent alternatives that can help you get through frightening situations. Let's look now at the potential danger in television advertising. Perhaps you never thought that TV ads could be dangerous!

Programs for kids advertise cereals, candy, toys, dolls, games, and amusement parks. And, of course, war games and war toys — including guns, cannons, soldiers, forts and tanks, as well as military uniforms, comics, movies and video games.

When you see ads on TV, do you want to buy those products? What attracts you to them? How are war toys advertised so that you want to own them? Did you know that the companies that make these products spend a lot of money to try to get you to buy them?

There are cigarette advertisers who spend over *$2 billion* a year in advertising trying to get people to smoke cigarettes, even though it has been proven, beyond a doubt, that cigarette smoking is extremely hazardous to our health. The law even requires a warning to be printed on packages of cigarettes to that effect. But manufacturers still try to get us to buy them.

What Can You Do?

There is a business theory called "supply and demand." It means that if you, the consumer, want something (demand), then someone or some company will probably try to make it and sell it to you (supply). If people stopped buying war toys and games, then the demand for them would be gone, and companies would stop making them. And if companies stopped making them, no one would be able to buy them!

If you believe, as I do, that playing with guns and other war toys is dangerous because it inspires us to think in a warlike way, there are some things you can do to discourage it.

1. **Know Your Rights.** A consumer is a person who buys products; you are a consumer, and you have certain rights as a consumer. Business aimed at kids is gigantic; business owners make *billions* of dollars from toys sold to children — so young people are an important consumer group. You can write to this address to find out more about your rights:

> Zillions
> 256 Washington Street
> Mt. Vernon, NY 10553
> Telephone: (914) 667-9400
> (Ask for their magazine, <u>Zillions</u>:
> Consumer Reports for Kids.)

2. **Refuse to Buy Harmful Products.** You can have an effect on manufacturers by not buying products you don't believe in. As a concerned consumer, you can tell your friends why you have decided not to buy these products, and you can ask them not to buy them as well. You can refuse gifts from friends and family that are war

oriented, or exchange them at the store where they were purchased.

3. **Contact Your Local Store Owner.** Tell your local store owner that you (and your friends and family, if they agree with you) would prefer that the store not carry certain products. Name the toys and games that you believe are not healthy for young people to play with.

4. **Make a List of Positive Toys and Games.** Offer suggestions to the store owner about the kinds of toys and games you would prefer to buy and what you like to play with — such as science sets, arts and crafts, building components, sports toys. In this way, you are not only explaining what you don't like, but you're offering the store owner alternatives to keep his business from losing sales. It's always helpful to think in terms of alternatives.

5. **Start a Petition.** Gather a list of names and addresses of people who agree with you. Send these petitions, explaining your concerns, to toy makers and government agencies.

6. **Contact War Toy Manufacturers.** Find the names and addresses of manufacturers and ask them to please stop making these toys. On the following page is an address to start your list...

G. I. Joe Manufacturers
Hasbro, Inc.
200 Narragansett Park Drive
Pawtucket, RI 02862
Telephone: (401) 431-8697

7. Find Special Interest Groups. Keep a record (names, addresses, telephone numbers) of groups that concern themselves with these issues. Here are some to start your list:

The Stop War Toys Campaign
P.O. Box 1093
Norwich, CT 06360
Telephone:
(203) 889-5337 or (203) 455-9621

War Resisters League
339 Lafayette Street
New York, NY 10012
Telephone: (212) 228-0450

National Coalition on Television Violence
P.O. Box 2157
Champagne, IL 61825
Telephone: (217) 384-1920

8. Make Telephone Calls. Contact organizations that support anti-war toy campaigns. (See sample conversation on page 140.) Also, call stores that carry these toys and ask them not to.

9. **Write Letters.** Write c/o the editor of local newspapers and encourage people not to buy war toys. (See sample letter following.)

10. **Protest and Picket.** Protest television stations broadcasting G.I. Joe cartoons or other war-promoting programs by letter writing and picketing.

11. **Organize Letter-Writing Parties.** Ask your teachers at school to organize an event to protest war toys, games and cartoons — to which parents and friends are invited. Write to war toy manufacturers and special interest groups.

If you come up with new ideas to change the policies of war toy manufacturers and advertisers, please write and let me know. I'd like to hear from you. (You'll find my address at the back of this book.)

Sample Telephone Call

"Hello, my name is _____ ,
and I'm _____ years old. I have an objection to some of the
toys and games that are coming into the marketplace for
young people like me. I'm putting together a petition to
protest the war games and guns manufactured by

_____ ,

and I'm wondering if I may come to your next meeting and
gather signatures for the cause. I can. Great. Please tell me
where it will be and what time. Thanks for your help.

Sample Letter

Hartley Haverty
1331 Homewood Avenue
Summerville, California 90031

September 30, 1990

Mr. Lawrence Laken   *(This is a fictitious name and address.)*
Battalion Toys, Inc.
100 West Corporal Avenue
Warville, Minnesota 55111

Dear Mr. Laken:

    I represent 15 schools in my particular county of California, and we have gathered 15,000 signatures to protest the guns and soldier games you have been manufacturing which we feel encourage children to think in warlike ways and promote warlike behavior. We feel strongly that these toys and games should no longer be manufactured, and we are determined to carry our campaign throughout the state of California. We have the support of our state senators and representatives.

    We don't want you to lose any sales or have to go out of business, so we have come up with some alternate games and toys we think could make you a lot of money, and we would be pleased to talk with you about them. We distributed a questionnaire in our 15 schools and 87% of the kids polled said they would buy these toys and games if they were for sale.

    Thank you for your consideration and concern about children. We look forward to hearing from you.

Sincerely,

Hartley Haverty

cc: Senator Alan Cranberry
     Representative Peter Wilbury

Chapter 14

ACTIVITIES AND EXERCISES

This chapter consists of activities and exercises you can do to help yourself become free of conditioned thinking, the source of conflict. The most important "activity" of all is to *understand* what is happening to you when you are in conflict. It will be to your advantage to look at your fear, listen to it, and begin to see where your conflict comes from. Once you understand what conflict is, you can explore how it comes about and begin to get free of it.

Inner Conflict Awareness Exercise

Conflict may not always be expressed by violence — as when one person strikes another. Conflict may come out as a disagreement with someone. Or conflict may remain inside as inner pain — for instance, when your feelings have been hurt and no one knows.

The following activity is an exercise in inner conflict awareness. You can do this activity by yourself, by writing down your answers on paper — or you can do it with others (from two to four people). If you're doing it with others, write down your responses privately, then share them afterwards.

1. Write on a piece of paper, "I believe..." and then write down whatever comes into your head first. Write 10 different responses.

2. Then write "I don't believe..." Again, write down whatever comes into your head, and repeat 10 times.

3. Now write, "I should..." Write down what comes to mind, and do this 10 times also.

4. Then write, "I shouldn't..." (10 times)

5. Now try, "I believe in..." (10 times)

6. Now write, "I don't believe in..." (10 times)

If you have been doing this with others, everyone takes a turn at sharing their responses. Compare your responses to those of your friends. Ask one another:

1. Why do you believe...?
2. Why don't you believe...?
3. Why do you think you should...?
4. Why do you think you shouldn't...?

What did you find out? Were some of your answers the same as those of your friends? Were some different? Were some opposite? Ask each other:

1. Where do your beliefs or "shoulds" or "shouldn'ts" come from? Can you remember the time when you first heard this belief? Was it at home? At school? From a friend or a relative?

2. Do you think you were born with these beliefs, or do you think you learned them?

3. Why do you think you were conditioned to believe these things?

The Shining Moment Game

Have you ever seen a Chinese finger puzzle? You put one finger in each end and pull. The harder you try to get out of the puzzle, the tighter its grip becomes. This is also true of the battle of good over evil. The harder you try to become "good" (whatever "good" means to you), the greater the struggle will seem to get rid of the "bad" (whatever "bad" means to you).

We all have moments when we shine and moments when we don't.

1. Write down three moments when you really shined.

_____ .

_____ .

_____ .

Example:

A. I cleaned my room before my mother asked me to and surprised her.
B. I climbed a tree to save my neighbor's cat, even though it was scary to climb so high.

C. I prevented a fight between myself and a classmate by encouraging her to talk things out.

2. Then write down three moments when you were not proud of your actions.

_____ .

_____ .

_____ .

Example:

A. I yelled at my father when he asked me to mow the lawn.
B. I bullied a kid into giving me a dollar.
C. I blamed my little sister for spilling milk on the carpet, when I actually did it.

Share these moments with classmates, friends or family. Everyone takes a turn telling about their shining or non-shining moments. Rather than judging your behavior as "good" or "bad," look at your attributes and imperfections, and see that you have both, just like every human being. Listen to the beliefs of your friends and family in the same way — *without judgment*.

When you look at beliefs without judging them, you become less "conditioned" in your behavior. Becoming aware of your beliefs and actions wakes you up to being responsible for what you do. And when you take responsibility for what you do, you feel strong and confident.

The Self-Consciousness Scale

Write down the answers, or share out loud with friends:

1. I think I am bad when I:

   _____

2. I think I am good when I:

   _____

3. People don't like me when I :

   _____

4. People like me when I:

   _____

5. I would like to be like (name a person):

   _____

6. I would not like to be like (name a person):

   _____

7. I don't like it when my (friends/parents/relatives/
   teachers) think I am:

   _____

8. I like it when my (friends/parents/relatives/teachers)
   think I am:

   _____

Discuss your responses with others in your class or in your family. Try to find out where you got your ideas about what it means to be "good" and why you feel the way you do.

The Detective Game

1. One person describes something that he/she is afraid of.

2. The next person gets one guess as to *why* the first person is afraid.

3. The first person confirms or denies the guess.

4. Every person in the room gets one guess, then every person gets a second guess, until someone gives an accurate description of why the first person is afraid.

5. If nobody guesses the reason why the first person is afraid of whatever he or she is afraid of, the first person then has to tell the real reason.

6. Then every person gets a chance to offer a suggestion on how to overcome that fear.

The Observation Game

1. One person is chosen to say something mean or cruel to another person.

2. The person to whom the cruel words are spoken must...

A. Listen to the cruel words;

B. Sit quietly and allow any images to come to mind;

C. Not do anything — just watch;

D. Breathe deeply;

E. Let the words come and go.

3. Remind the person that images and words are not able to hurt on their own. The idea is to face the images and words — and realize that they don't have control over you, unless you let them.

4. Give everyone in the room the opportunity to have mean or cruel words spoken to him or to her, and to work through the feelings that come up as a result.

The "I See/I Imagine Game"

This is a very simple game that can demonstrate the difference between what you *actually* see and what you *imagine* you see. This game can show you how conditioned you are and how what you think you see is just that — what you *think* you see, and not what *is actually happening.*

For example, if I look at you and see that your eyes are filled with water, I might say, "Why are you crying?" What I see is water in your eyes; what I imagine is that you are crying out of sadness. But perhaps the truth is that you just cut up some onions, or that something else is irritating your eyes, or that you were laughing at a funny joke just before I saw you. The point is to see the difference between what you imagine is the "truth" and what is actually occurring. Do you see the importance of this? If you act out of your imagination, can you see how conflict can be created?

Here are some ways to play this game. (You may be able to think of other ways.) One person starts off. He or she looks at another person, and says — for example:

"I *see* that you are frowning."
"I *imagine* that you're angry."

- OR -

"I *see* that your shirt is ripped."
"I *imagine* that you were in a fight."

- OR -

"I *see* that you are smiling."
"I *imagine* that you are happy about your report card.

Each person in the group (three or four people are a good number) comments on any other person in the group. Then discuss the misunderstandings that may have occurred.

Another way to play this game is remember incidents in the day that happened to you that caused conflict. Say to another or others (or to yourself if you are playing the game alone):

"Today I saw＿＿＿＿＿＿＿＿＿＿＿＿＿＿＿＿＿＿＿＿＿ ,

and I imagined ＿＿＿＿＿＿＿＿＿＿＿＿＿＿＿＿＿＿＿＿＿

＿＿＿＿＿＿＿＿＿＿＿＿＿＿＿＿＿＿＿＿＿＿＿＿＿ .

This caused confusion or conflict because:

_____

_____ .

Example:

Today I *saw* Judy storming down the hall towards me, and I *imagined* that she was angry with me.

This caused conflict because I called out to her, "Leave me alone!" and then I walked away with my friends.

If you later discovered the truth about what you saw, you can add: The truth is that...

_____ .

(For example: Judy was upset because her mother yelled at her in the car before school.)

Can you see that what we imagine we see may not be what is actually happening?! Much of what we imagine, what we think we see, comes out of our conditioning. Like a good detective, we want to find out the facts about what is really going on. So, we must be careful to check what we imagine against what the real truth is. If we do this, then chances are we will not be acting out of conditioned thinking. Therefore, we will be less likely to create conflict.

Can you think of situations in your life when you acted on what you *imagined* another person was saying or doing, and how this caused confusion or conflict? Can you think of incidents where groups or nations imagined certain things to be true that were not really true, and how this caused conflict? It is important to be aware of how conditioned thinking can cloud perception.

The "Love the Bully" Game

This can be played by two or more people. One person roleplays the bully, and another the victim, while the others watch. Eventually, everyone takes a turn at being both bully and victim. Read these lines as if you are in a play.

Roleplay:

Bully: "Hey you! Give me your wallet, or I'll beat you to a pulp!"

Victim: *(Immediately thinks of Bully's name and treats him as a friend.)* "Hi, Ralph. Aren't you Ralph Wilson? I saw you catch a great fast ball in the stadium last week. You were terrific."

Bully: "Never mind the game, punk. I heard you have a lot of money. Gimme it!"

Victim: "I don't know where you heard that. Aren't you from Minnesota? I have a cousin back there. Maybe you know him. He plays baseball too."

Bully: "I'm talking money, pal, not Minnesota!"

Victim: "Listen, I don't want to fight. I don't have a lot of money, but if you need some, why don't you talk to the coach. I hear they sometimes give loans to students at this school."

The victim remains cool and calm and admits he does not want to fight, which gives the bully nothing to fight about.

After you have roleplayed these characters, ask one another these questions:

1. How did it make you feel to play the victim?
2. How did it make you feel to play the bully?
3. How did it feel to watch someone being bullied?

Then make up your own Bully/Victim dialogue.

The Fear Game

Choose some sentences or statements that bring fear into the minds of the participants, such as: "You're a skinny runt, and I'm going to beat you up!" or "Give me your money, or I'll wreck your bicycle."

Discuss the feelings that run through you when you hear statements like these. Some examples are:

1. "I just want to run away."
2. "I want to punch that guy's lights out!"
3. "This kid is really uptight; maybe I can calm him down."

Talk about whether these reactions are:

A. The "fight" response
B. The "flight" response
C. Becoming aware and reasoning response

The Roleplay Game

Take one of the new words you've learned in this book and create a roleplay situation that explains the word. Pick a partner for the roleplay. Some of the words than can be played:

Prejudgment	Tradition
Identification	Habit
Repression	Value
Projection	Custom
Scapegoating	Attitude

Example: Prejudgment

Dale: There goes Dan. I've never seen such a stuck-up kid.

Pat: I don't think he's stuck-up.

Dale: Yes, he is. He just moved into the neighborhood and he never talks to anyone.

Pat: He talked to me yesterday.

Dale: Oh, yeah? What about?

Pat: I said hi and welcomed him to our school, and he said, "Thanks." Then he smiled and blushed a little and walked away. I think he's just shy.

If you can create roleplay situations that demonstrate the meaning of the above words, you will develop a clearer sense of what the words mean and become more *aware* in such situations when they arise. The more aware you become, the more likely you are to use nonviolent alternatives, and the less likely you are to create conflict.

A SPECIAL NOTE TO THE YOUNG READER

Thank you for reading this book. I hope that you have begun to understand conditioning and how it creates conflict and violence, and what you can do about it. I find that it's a wonderful experience to be free of conditioned thinking and living; I feel much happier and freer when I am. This is so important in living a really sane and intelligent life. I'm glad we could share in this journey together. If you have any questions or suggestions in response to this book, you can write to me at this address:

Terrence Webster-Doyle
Atrium Publications
P. O. Box 938
Ojai, California 93024-0938

I would very much like to hear from you.

With care,

Terrence Webster-Doyle

Terrence Webster-Doyle

P.S. The last part of this book is for your parents, teachers or counselors. You are welcome to continue reading, or you can stop here and consider what you've just read. There's a lot to think about!

A Message to Parents, Teachers, Counselors or Anyone Who Works or Lives with Young People

The fundamental intention of this book is to help young people understand what causes conflict in their relationships and offer them ways to deal with it. Some people think that we cannot fundamentally affect what creates conflict. I feel we cannot only understand how we create conflict in our lives, we can do something about it.

The fundamental cause of conflict in relationship is what I call "conditioning." This is a process of programming behavior that causes us to act in predetermined, habitual ways. An obvious example of this is found in our training of animals. Through punishment and reward, a trainer will "condition" an animal to act in a certain manner; most of us are familiar with the experiments involving Pavlov's dogs which demonstrated the effect of using stimuli to elicit predictable responses.

We all condition young people to act in habitual ways. In certain situations, programming behavior is necessary. For example, we teach our children to stop for a red traffic light. The reason is obvious: We don't want them to get hurt by a moving vehicle. But there are destructive ramifications of certain forms of conditioning. Aldous Huxley, in *Brave New World* and *Brave New World Revisited*, depicted a world controlled by the conscious manipulation of behavior to breed a world of people who would willingly live under the rules and regulations of a select few in power.

This book, *Fighting the Invisible Enemy*, is meant to show young people what conditioning is, how it comes about, and why certain kinds of conditioning can be dangerous. It is my view that conditioning is the fundamental cause of conflict, individually and socially, and, therefore, is the seed of war. The more I look into the structure of conditioning, the more disastrous the effects I see. Our work, our relationships, and even our "play" are conditioned to some extent. We live habitually, acting out time-worn beliefs that have been handed down generation after

157

generation. Some of these are based on intelligent values, traditions and attitudes, and some are not. But when they are learned by rote and go unquestioned, they can be destructive to human intelligence and sensitivity.

There is no question that we must learn to live ethically and sanely, but how do we go about this? In our desire to bring about "good," "moral" behavior, we have brought about the opposite, creating tremendous conflict and suffering in the process.

The Root of Conflict

The basic premise of this book is that the root of conflict is fear: Fear creates the conditioned response, and is a major component of the "invisible enemy." If we look at ourselves, we can see that we are creatures of habit. We are also "animals" with certain biological urges and instincts. These urges, or instincts, such as hunger and sex, are the result of our "biological conditioning." When we encounter a situation that causes us to feel fear, we come face-to-face with yet another biological reaction — the "fight or flight" instinct. You can see this instinct at work in your own home, when the cat meets up with the dog. For a second, they freeze. Then one of them either races away or makes a move to strike at the other. This "fight or flight" mechanism in humans resides in what we call the "old brain" — the brain we've inherited from our primitive ancestors. Fear triggers this mechanism.

As an educator and psychology teacher, I have been interested in understanding the social effects of the "fight or flight" mechanism. I have been exploring whether this might be one of the major underlying factors of conflict — both individually and globally. For years, I have also been studying the Martial Art of Karate, and through this practice have developed a way to circumvent the "fight or flight" reaction. I notice that when young people are confronted with a physically threatening situation, they usually react by either fighting or running — or cowering. My own youth was no different. Growing up just outside New York City, I was neither a fighter nor a fast runner. I allowed myself to be intimidated; this became my conditioned response. Later in life, I learned simple psychological alternatives that could turn a potentially threatening situation into a peaceful one, with no one "losing face."

Having been both a teacher of psychology and an instructor of Martial Arts, I began to see how I could combine the skills of both into an approach that would give young people the confidence (through acquiring self-defense skills) to handle a physical threat, and the psychological ability (through roleplaying) to dissipate hostility. It's so simple and it works!

When children can defend themselves, both physically and psychologically, then a threat to their physical well-being no longer presents them with only two alternatives: "fight or flight." Instead, they have a sense of confidence, and it is this confidence which helps them through their fear. Faced now with a threat, these children enter a "space" or a "pause" in which their minds can creatively determine nonviolent steps to take to resolve the situation. It is fascinating to watch a once timid or a once aggressive child become able to handle a threatening situation with skill. In the face of conflict, the choices now available are not solely based on the biological conditioned response of "fight or flight." Fighting can cause physical pain; fleeing can cause emotional pain. Dealing creatively with this limited, conditioned approach creates the possibility of coping rationally with a potentially hostile situation. When fear is lessened, the mind is able to reason. Reasoning dissolves conflict and opens the way to learning.

Another Kind of Threat

There is another kind of threat to our children that concerns me. Statistics show that most children watch 30 to 50 hours of TV per week, and 30,000 to 40,000 commercials per year! If this is accurate, the visual violence of television will assault their senses approximately 25,000 times with murder, assault and rape by the time they reach the age of 18. With the additional influence of violent movies, comics and magazines, our children are saturated with terrifying images.

Doesn't it make sense that the frequent witnessing of violence through television would significantly affect a child's behavior? Violent

159

images trigger fear, which then triggers the "fight or flight" mechanism, just as if the child were being actually physically threatened. The "fight or flight" mechanism, which is biological and involuntary, cannot differentiate between a physical or psychological threat. It merely reads: "Threat!" As a result, children demonstrate one of two responses: (1) they have nightmares, or (2) they develop a need to take on a "warrior image" to keep their fears at bay.

When I was a child in the 1940s, there was an unwritten code of ethics that violence portrayed on the screen or in print was not to be "too scary." There was always a degree of make-believe to violence then. We willingly suspended our disbelief so that we could vicariously enter the exciting world that only movies and magazines could offer. And it was fun! I remember, for example, being frightened by Abbott and Costello meeting Frankenstein, but there was humor and pathos in those scary scenes.

Then sometime around the Vietnam War, we stepped over the line, and violence became very real. Chainsaw hackers, axe killers, and other extremely realistic portrayals of violence filled our screens and minds. Our ability to choose to suspend disbelief was overwhelmed. Fact became difficult to differentiate from fantasy. "Social paranoia" began to take root. As I see it, the tremendous fears, and the defensive and offensive attitudes that permeate our culture today, come from being confronted with so much violence.

This current house of horrors in which we live has a long developmental history. War has been a commonplace occurrence for thousands of years. Religious intimidations threatening hell, fire, damnation and a vengeful God are a dramatic form of behavior control. The images offered by TV, movies and magazines are recent additions to factors that have conditioned us through centuries to be victimized by hostile threats and aggression.

As a parent, teacher and school director, I am vitally concerned with what affects our children's lives. Young people *learn* how to be violent. "American Heroes" and "action toys" for young boys, and now girls, present unrealistic, unhealthy role models.

Some people assert that only specialists — psychologists, teachers, politicians, historians, sociologists, religious leaders — can understand the complex problems of relationship, that this is beyond the average person's grasp. This perspective is sad and demeaning, and I strongly disagree. It was the young child who saw that the Emperor was really wearing no clothes, and was able to speak the truth. I believe the young mind can see things as they truly are. I have witnessed young people nonintellectually, nonjudgmentally observe their own thoughts, and come to an understanding of how their beliefs have caused conflict in their lives. I know they can develop this awareness.

We adults are often so conditioned that it is difficult to simply look. Our vested interests of wealth, status and power make it difficult for us to hear simple truths. The obvious childlike observations that pierce the complexity of our protective, defensive, intellectual minds are threatening because the status quo is challenged thereby. If we do take a hard look at what we are doing, we are afraid that we will have to change.

We are the ones who create conflict. We are, therefore, the ones to stop it. The only way to stop it is to understand it — to honestly examine the underlying causes of conflict. The momentum of society at the present time is to condition young people to "go for it," to carry on in basically the same aggressive, self-centered way their ancestors have for centuries. But we are approaching a time in history when we will have to change our ways or perish. This is not an overly emotional statement; it is a brutal fact. We obviously have the technological military power to destroy ourselves.

To survive, we can no longer exploit each other. The world is now such that we have to fully depend on one another and work together. We must, therefore, educate our children to consider the problems of relationship, examine the symptoms of conflict, and understand its causes. Our schools must address this crisis, and we must talk about it at home.

A framework for understanding — for stimulating enquiry, to encourage "intelligent understanding" — is long overdue. The word "intelligence," which is most often limited to mean "I.Q.," also involves insight: the capacity to perceive the nature of things. It is my observation that this component of intelligence has been neglected in education. The way for learning to become whole is to integrate an understanding of ourselves in relationship with the academic school curricula, so that education reflects understanding. In this way, we can enjoy, with our children, whole, healthy lives.

ABOUT THE AUTHOR

Terrence Webster-Doyle was Founder and Director of three independent schools and has taught at the secondary, community college and university levels in Education, Psychology and Philosophy. He has worked in Juvenile Delinquency Prevention and has developed counseling programs for teenagers. He has earned a doctorate degree in Psychology, has produced numerous conferences and workshops on New Directions in Education, and was the Director of The Center for Educational Alternatives in Northern California. Currently, he is Co-director of a secondary school whose intent is to explore psychological conditioning, and is working on a series of children's books exploring this theme.

Other books for young people by Terrence Webster-Doyle:

Facing the Double-Edged Sword:
The Art of Karate for Young People*

Tug of War:
Peace Through Understanding Conflict for Young People

Why is Everybody Always Picking on Me?:
A Guide to Handling Bullies for Young People

Books for adults by Terrence Webster-Doyle:

Growing Up Sane: *Understanding the Conditioned Mind*

Brave New Child: *Education for the 21st Century*

The Religious Impulse: *A Quest for Innocence*

Peace — The Enemy of Freedom: *The Myth of Nonviolence*

Karate: *The Art of Empty Self*

One Encounter, One Chance: *The Essence of Take Nami Do Karate***

*Finalist: Benjamin Franklin Award • Winner: Award of Excellence, Ventura Ad Society
**Finalist, Benjamin Franklin Award — Psychology/Self-Help

ABOUT THE PUBLISHER

Atrium Publications concerns itself with fundamental issues which prevent understanding and cooperation in human affairs. Starting with the fact that our minds are conditioned by our origin of birth, our education and our experiences, Atrium Publications' intent is to bring this issue of conditioning to the forefront of our awareness. Observation of the fact of conditioning — becoming directly aware of the movement of thought and action — brings us face-to-face with the actuality of ourselves. Seeing who we actually are, not merely what we think we are, reveals the potential for a transformation of our ways of being and relating.

If you would like more information, please write or call us. We enjoy hearing from people who read our books and appreciate your comments.

Atrium Publications
P. O. Box 938
Ojai, California 93024-0938
Telephone: (805) 646-0488
(Call collect for book order information.)

WE'VE MOVED
PO Box 816
Middlebury, VT 05753
(802) 388-0922

ABOUT THE ARTIST

Rod Cameron was born in 1948 in Chicago, Illinois, but has lived in Southern California most of his life. He studied painting with the "Dick and Jane" illustrator, Keith Ward, and at the Otis/Parsons School of Design in Los Angeles, California.

In 1985, Rod Cameron founded East/West Arts, Inc., a design and art studio in Ventura, California. His work has been shown on major network television and has received 17 awards for illustrative excellence.